# The Executive Guide to Directing Projects: within a PRINCE2™ and MSP® Environment

London: TSO

Published by TSO (The Stationery Office) and available from:

**Online**
**www.tsoshop.co.uk**

**Mail, Telephone, Fax & E-mail**
TSO
PO Box 29, Norwich, NR3 1GN
Telephone orders/General enquiries: 0870 600 5522
Fax orders: 0870 600 5533
E-mail: customer.services@tso.co.uk
Textphone 0870 240 3701

**TSO@Blackwell and other Accredited Agents**

**Customers can also order publications from:**
TSO Ireland
16 Arthur Street, Belfast BT1 4GD
Tel 028 9023 8451 Fax 028 9023 5401

First published 2009

ISBN 9780113311897

Printed in the United Kingdom for The Stationery Office
P002333060   c10   12/09   959

# Contents

# List of figures

# List of tables

# Foreword

PRINCE2™ is established internationally as the standard method for project management in more than 20,000 organizations worldwide. The practitioner base continues to grow and is instrumental in the process of continual improvement that has kept the method at the forefront of project management for in excess of 20 years.

Time after time, the role of senior management has been shown to be critical in the success, or failure, of projects. The latest version of PRINCE2, published by TSO in 2009 (*Managing Successful Projects with PRINCE2*), acknowledged this by publishing a separate guide for managers in senior positions in a project governance structure (*Directing Successful Projects with PRINCE2*). This guide describes what is required of Project Board members, and in particular the Project Executive, in being accountable for the project and demonstrating visible ownership. It shows how they can optimize their interventions in the project management process to improve the probability of successful project delivery.

But there is a bigger picture. Individual projects deliver elements of an organization's overall business change strategy and have to coordinate with other delivery projects in a programme or compete for funds and resources in the organization's overall portfolio of change. This briefing provides senior managers with the key information they need for the successful delivery of their programmes or projects and should help them to ensure that their programmes or projects contribute towards the organization's business strategy.

Jonathan Shebioba

Director of Best Management Practice

*Office of Government Commerce*

# Acknowledgements

The Office of Government Commerce (OGC) acknowledges with thanks the contributions of Bob Patterson, the lead author of the guide, and Jane Chittenden as editor. In addition, OGC would like to recognize the contribution of Andy Murray, the lead author for the PRINCE2 2009 Refresh, and the following individuals who acted as reviewers:

| | |
|---|---|
| Tom Abram | WS Atkins |
| Mike Acaster | Office of Government Commerce |
| Trevor Band | |
| Terry Dailey | Deliverables Management Consultants |
| Adrian Kent | National School of Government |
| Ian Santry | Home Office |
| Rod Sowden | Aspire |

# Introduction

1

# 1 Introduction

## 1.1 THE PURPOSE OF THIS GUIDE

The effectiveness with which organizations are capable of commissioning and directing projects is fundamental to their ability to adapt in constantly changing circumstances and to undertake large-scale innovation.

Projects in Controlled Environments (PRINCE2), established as one of the most widely used project management methods, is part of a wider framework of OGC best practice that addresses how inter-related projects are best coordinated and controlled in programmes, and how an organization should actively plan and manage its overall portfolio of change initiatives.

This guide is intended for senior executives involved in directing projects. Its purpose is to provide:

- Practical advice on directing projects using PRINCE2
- An understanding of the wider context of project delivery, including programme and portfolio management.

## 1.2 USING THE GUIDE

It is assumed that readers may already have some high-level awareness of PRINCE2 but a detailed knowledge is not required.

The guide is structured as follows:

- Chapter 1 (this chapter) addresses the defining characteristics of projects, explains the relationship with programmes and portfolios, and introduces PRINCE2
- Chapter 2 examines the senior management (Project Board) roles
- Chapter 3 describes the duties and behaviours expected of Project Board members
- Chapter 4 summarizes the key Project Board activities
- Chapter 5 addresses the wider context of programmes and portfolios
- Chapter 6 illustrates the use of PRINCE2 and other OGC guidance as a diagnostic tool for troubleshooting.

The detailed sources for the PRINCE2 method are the two OGC guides: *Directing Successful Projects with PRINCE2* (TSO, 2009) and *Managing Successful Projects with PRINCE2* (TSO, 2009). This guide also draws from OGC's programme management manual, *Managing Successful Programmes* (TSO, 2007).

For precise definitions of the terms used in this guide, please consult the Glossary. Otherwise, the OGC *PRINCE2 Pocketbook* (TSO, 2009) is highly recommended as a handy and definitive reference publication.

A summary of other relevant OGC guidance is given in Appendix A.

## 1.3 ABOUT PROJECTS

In common usage, the term 'project' can be applied to a range of activities varying in scale from building a small-scale IT system to building the Channel Tunnel. So what do these two project examples (building an IT system and building the Channel Tunnel) have in common? And what distinguishes them from other forms of activity (specifically, 'business as usual' services)? Consider the following:

- Projects are the means by which we introduce change (the new IT system/Channel Tunnel)
- They are temporary (once the change is implemented, they finish)
- They are almost always cross-functional: that is, they involve people with specialist skills ('suppliers') developing something (the 'product' or 'products') for other people (who will be the 'users')
- Each project is unique in some way (unlike a production line or a regular service function)
- The previous four characteristics combine to make projects generally more risky.

It can be seen that the project phase is often considered part of a wider 'product lifecycle' – for example, the IT system, the Channel Tunnel, a vehicle model, a computer application, a pharmaceutical product etc. – as shown in the (simplified) diagram in Figure 1.1.

## 1.4 PORTFOLIOS AND PROGRAMMES

The extent of management required for a small project (such as the IT system mentioned above) will be very different from that for a very large one (such as the Channel Tunnel). More precise terms are needed to define the different scales of management framework required.

Few projects are standalone; most projects are linked in some way with others being delivered at the same time. For example, a project to deliver a new IT system could be linked to a project for staff training and another for updating the

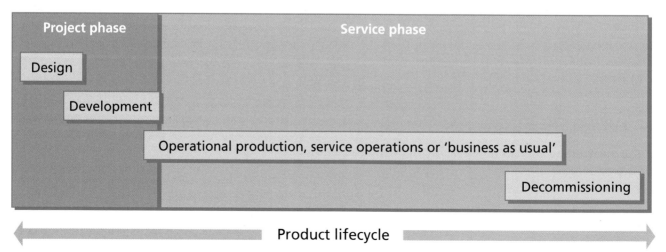

*Figure 1.1 The place of the project in the product lifecycle*

IT infrastructure; so it usually makes sense to coordinate the effort in a programme of linked projects.

In many organizations, programmes and projects will be delivered in a complex multi-project environment, where there will be competing priorities for scarce resources. There will be inter-relationships between projects and programmes – such as the impact on one project if another fails. In this context there is often also contention when resources are being shared between projects and services. The sponsoring organization or unit must manage its overall portfolio of investment in programmes and services.

> **Hints and tips**
>
> Although in the past, PRINCE2 has often been introduced to good effect on its own, it is generally recommended that the best approach to 'embedding' the full portfolio, programme and project framework in an organization is 'top-down', adopting portfolio management as early as possible. This makes it easier to identify projects that should be cancelled because they are inconsistent with the portfolio strategy and/ or low priority.

The hierarchy of terms used in the OGC best-practice framework is outlined in Figure 1.2. Services represent 'business as usual' and are therefore outside the scope of this guide.

At the portfolio level, management decides on the optimum balance of services, change programmes and projects for the business or business unit (bearing in mind the resources available), and then determines the priorities and supervises the

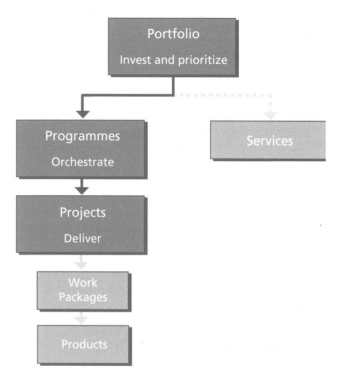

**Figure 1.2 The portfolio, programme and project hierarchy**

overall effort. Portfolio management (PfM) is OGC's recommended approach for managing portfolios.

At the programme level, management defines the strategic outcomes and benefits required, then orchestrates the delivery effort. *Managing Successful Programmes* (TSO, 2007) (MSP®) is OGC's recommended approach for managing programmes.

At the project level, managers plan and control the delivery of change (and the focus is on products). PRINCE2 is OGC's recommended approach for managing projects.

Specialist engineering models (or project lifecycles) for specific types of project (construction, IT, pharmaceuticals etc.) can easily be integrated with the PRINCE2 management framework simply by identifying and defining the specialist products that the project must create (see Figure 1.3). PRINCE2 provides effective techniques for doing this, and many industry-specific standard project lifecycles are already well established.

The PRINCE2 project management method is used in more than 150 countries around the world, and its take-up grows daily. Originally developed by the OGC for the UK public sector, it is widely considered as the leading methodology in project management. More than 20,000 organizations are already benefiting from its pioneering and trusted approach.

For more information about PRINCE2's principles, themes and processes, and the benefits of using PRINCE2, see Appendix B.

## 1.5 WHAT IS PRINCE2?

PRINCE2 is a fully integrated framework of best practice for managing projects. It is expressed in terms of principles, themes and processes. Guidance is also provided for adopting PRINCE2 as a corporate standard (embedding) and adapting the method to fit different types of project (tailoring), emphasizing the method's flexibility.

PRINCE2 can be applied to any project regardless of scale, type, sponsoring organization(s), geography or culture: it is truly generic. PRINCE2 achieves this by isolating the management aspects of project work (team organization, planning and controls) from the specialist aspects such as design, construction etc.

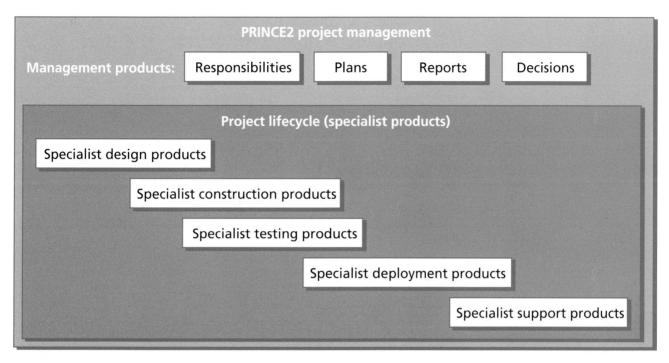

*Figure 1.3  Generic project management with specific specialist application*

# The role of senior management in PRINCE2

2

# 2 The role of senior management in PRINCE2

This chapter explains the PRINCE2 Organization theme and more specifically the roles of the senior managers involved in a PRINCE2 project as Project Board members.

## 2.1 THE PRINCE2 ORGANIZATION

The PRINCE2 Organization theme is integrated with the other PRINCE2 themes to set up an unambiguous framework of responsibilities.

Figure 2.1 shows the Project Board in the context of the overall PRINCE2 project management team structure.

Project Board members are appointed by corporate or programme management and are accountable for the success (or failure) of the project concerned.

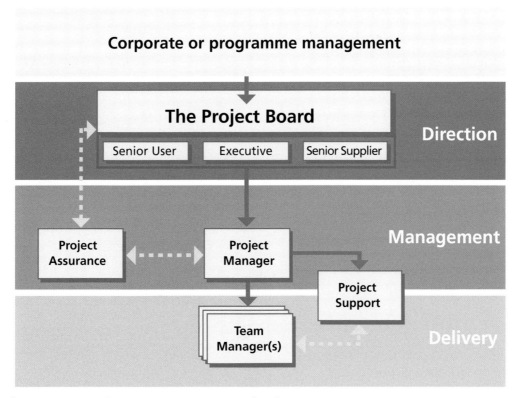

*Figure 2.1  The PRINCE2 project management organization*

**Hints and tips**

The PRINCE2 project organization is a temporary ('matrix') structure. Project Board members will also be senior managers in the sponsoring organization(s). The extent of their business 'line' responsibilities is usually much wider than the project. They can rarely afford to get involved in the detail of every project for which they are responsible, so it is critically important that the project work can be delegated effectively.

In PRINCE2, the Project Board delegates the management of the project to the Project Manager in a series of stages, each based on an approved Stage Plan. If the Project Manager can deliver a stage within the tolerances defined by the Project Board (and included in the plan), there is no need for the Project Board members to maintain continuous close contact with the project work.

The stage boundaries are the major control milestones for the project, and Project Board reviews are held at these points to:

- Consider whether the Project Manager has delivered the previous stage successfully
- Review the continued overall viability of the project
- Approve a plan for the next stage.

The PRINCE2 processes provide other checks and balances but, essentially, this is how senior managers on the Project Board fulfil the PRINCE2 principle of 'managing by exception'.

## 2.2 PROJECT BOARD COMPOSITION

As indicated in Figure 2.1, all Project Board members fulfil one of three distinct roles:

- Executive – ultimately accountable
- Senior User
- Senior Supplier.

This represents the practical application of the PRINCE2 principle that a project always involves three primary stakeholder interests – those of the business investors, the users of the project's products and the suppliers of the products (Figure 2.2).

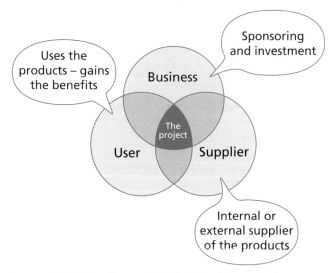

**Figure 2.2 The three stakeholder interests in a project**

The project will only succeed if:

- The products work – they have to be technically reliable and capable of operational maintenance (Senior Supplier's responsibility)
- The products also meet the users' requirements and enable the intended benefits to be realized (Senior User's responsibility)
- The overall return for the investment meets business expectations (Project Executive's business accountability).

As all three interests need to be satisfied, all three must be represented in the decision-making processes.

Consequently, Project Board members are responsible for Project Assurance from all three perspectives. However, they usually delegate some of this responsibility to other people (a Project Assurance function) who are independent of the project team (as shown in Figure 2.1).

The Project Board is also responsible for communication between the project and the stakeholders external to the project team (for example, corporate and programme management).

**Hints and tips**

Project Boards do not always consist of three members. The range of user and supplier interests may suggest the need for more than one Senior User and/or Senior Supplier, although there is only one Project Executive.

The Project Board is primarily a decision-making function, so it is preferable to have no more than five members. Other senior managers may attend Project Board meetings, either to observe or to offer specialist contributions, but it is only the Project Board members who make decisions.

### 2.2.1 The Executive

The Executive's role is to ensure that the project is focused throughout its life on achieving its business objectives and the forecast benefits. The Executive has to ensure that the project gives value for money, ensuring a cost-effective approach to the project, balancing the demands of the business, users and suppliers.

The Executive is appointed by corporate or programme management during the pre-project process, Starting up a Project. The role of the Executive is assigned to one individual, so that there is a single point of accountability for the project. The Executive is then responsible for appointing the rest of the project management team, including the other members of the Project Board.

Throughout the project, the Executive is responsible for the Business Case and needs to be able to take a balanced view on behalf of the wider organization.

**Hints and tips**

If the project is part of a programme, programme management will usually appoint some or all of the Project Board members.

### 2.2.2 The Senior User

The Senior User is responsible for:

- Committing user resources
- Ensuring that users' needs are accurately specified
- Ensuring that the solution will satisfy users' needs and contribute towards realizing the benefits intended for the business
- Communicating between the users and the project team.

The Senior User must be able to make decisions on behalf of those groups who will use or gain benefit from the project's products.

It is important to understand that, in practice, Senior Users are likely to be responsible for realizing the benefits for the business and this will probably involve 'business as usual' commitments after the end of the project.

**Hints and tips**

The Senior User may also represent the interests of those who will maintain the specialist products of the project after closure – but this is not always the case.

A Senior Supplier may instead be responsible for representing the interests of those who will maintain the project's products after closure (for example, when an external supplier is contracted for maintenance and support).

What matters is that long-term operations, service and support interests are represented appropriately on the Project Board from the outset.

**Hints and tips**

In large or complex projects there may be several discrete user stakeholders and/or supplier interests – too many to accommodate in a manageable Project Board. In these circumstances, user and/or supplier Advisory Boards can be set up, chaired respectively by the Senior User or the Senior Supplier.

As with a delegated Project Assurance role, Advisory Boards do not have any accountability for the project, but they do provide valuable support and guidance for Project Board members by helping to agree a coherent approach for the stakeholder group concerned.

Advisory Boards may also usefully double as a form of Project Assurance.

### 2.2.3 The Senior Supplier

The Senior Supplier represents the interests of those designing, developing, facilitating, procuring and implementing the project's products. He or she must be able to make decisions on behalf of those providing the expertise or resources to create the products.

This role is accountable for the quality of products delivered and for the technical integrity of the project. The responsibilities of the role include:

- Committing all required supplier resources to the project
- Ensuring that proposals for designing and developing the products are feasible and realistic.

# Project Board duties and behaviours

3

# 3  Project Board duties and behaviours

Before examining the Project Board's decision-making processes, it is necessary to be aware of the underlying duties and behaviours required of the members. This is an important factor in project success; surveys frequently cite lack of executive/senior management support as one of the top causes of project failure.

The duties of the Project Board are to:

■ Be accountable for the project
■ Provide unified direction
■ Delegate effectively
■ Facilitate cross-functional integration
■ Commit resources
■ Ensure effective decision making
■ Support the Project Manager
■ Ensure effective communication.

Each of these duties is discussed below.

## 3.1  BE ACCOUNTABLE FOR THE PROJECT

The Project Board is accountable for the success (or failure) of the project.

Being accountable means accepting and demonstrating ownership of the project. The Project Executive retains ultimate decision-making authority, but there is also an obligation on Senior User(s) and Senior Supplier(s) to ensure that the interests of their respective stakeholders are properly considered.

For instance, Senior User(s) are accountable for ensuring that the products of the project will enable the intended benefits to be realized operationally. If this does not happen, the project may be considered a 'success' on closure without ever subsequently enabling the benefits originally intended.

Senior Supplier(s) are accountable for ensuring that the products of the project are reliable, properly integrated, can be maintained efficiently etc. If this does not happen, the later stages of the project are likely to be fraught with problems, with repeated failures – or the benefits might be offset by operational maintenance difficulties after project closure.

It is part of the Project Executive's responsibility to ensure that the other Project Board members are selected carefully and perform their roles effectively. Consequently, the Project Executive must have sufficient authority in the project to make decisions.

Project Board members are responsible for ensuring that people with the right skills and experience are involved in the team and, particularly, in any Project Assurance roles.

**Hints and tips**

Where projects are managed as part of a programme, programme level managers (such as the programme manager and/or a business change manager) may also be appointed to Project Board roles for one or more of the projects in the programme. In effect, the project and programme governance structures overlap.

This type of integration promotes consistency of direction but care should be taken to preserve the authority of the Project Executive. Programme managers acting as Project Executives, for instance, may not have much management seniority outside their programme roles. If other Project Board members out-rank the Executive in the line structures of the business, it will prove difficult for the Executive to exert the necessary authority.

## 3.2 PROVIDE UNIFIED DIRECTION

Project Board members must provide unified direction.

Unified direction is about teamwork at Project Board level. While each Project Board member has accountability for satisfying the interests of a particular stakeholder category, it is crucial that a cohesive overall direction for the project is agreed and communicated.

As far as possible, Project Board members should defer to each other's areas of accountability and work together to achieve mutually agreed solutions. Project Board members should resolve issues by focusing on their likely impact on business benefits and then communicate the outcome in a way that minimizes any potential for friction.

If unified direction breaks down, and Project Board members communicate perceptibly different agendas, the effect is very rapidly translated into reduced momentum and/or conflicting activity at the project team level, with a serious probability of failure.

Unified direction applies regardless of whether the project concerns a commercial customer/supplier relationship or whether the users and suppliers are both internal to the same organization.

## 3.3 DELEGATE EFFECTIVELY

Project Board members must delegate effectively, using the PRINCE2 organizational structure and controls.

Several aspects of PRINCE2 are designed to promote effective delegation, such as the:

- Framework of roles and responsibilities in the project management team
- Plans designed to meet the needs of managers at different levels.

A key feature of PRINCE2 is the delegation of the day-to-day management of the project to the Project Manager on a stage-by-stage basis.

PRINCE2 projects are divided into a succession of management stages (time periods that, unlike the various technical activities such as design and construction, should never overlap). Stages bring benefits both in planning and progress control.

### 3.3.1 The 'stage contract'

To understand how PRINCE2 expects the Project Board to delegate the management of stage activity to a Project Manager, the Project Board should view the Stage Plan as a 'notional contract'.

The terms of this notional contract are outlined in the tinted box.

> **The stage contract**
>
> The Project Board undertakes, collectively, to:
>
> ■ Provide overall direction
> ■ Commit the resources in the plan.
>
> The Project Manager undertakes, subject to approved tolerances, to:
>
> ■ Deliver the stage products
> ■ Meet the product quality criteria
> ■ Deliver within the stage budget
> ■ Meet the target completion date.

This form of delegation requires a degree of trust between the Project Board members and the Project Manager, but PRINCE2 also provides checks and balances.

■ The Project Board will normally require the Project Manager to produce Highlight Reports at intervals throughout a stage to confirm that progress remains on track.

■ The Project Board members may use Project Assurance measures to confirm that their various stakeholder interests are being safeguarded at the working level (for example, part-time assurance roles or periodic independent checks). Peer reviews such as OGC's Gateway™ reviews are very effective as independent checks of project progress (see Appendix A for more information about Gateway reviews).

These arrangements enable the PRINCE2 project to progress as a series of stage contracts, minimizing the need for formal Project Board meetings.

> **Hints and tips**
>
> Where projects are managed as part of a programme, a notional contract similar to the stage contract described above will exist between the programme management and the Project Board. This is initially defined in the Project Brief and then subsequently in the Business Case and project-level tolerances.

### 3.3.2 Exceptions and escalation

This pattern of control can only work if there is also an understanding of what the Project Manager must do if things do not go to plan – that is, when an exception arises.

The way PRINCE2 handles 'exceptions' (departures from the approved plans) depends on the implementation of tolerances. Typically, tolerances are the levels of deviation permissible (above and below a plan's target for time and cost) before issues must be escalated to the next (higher) level of management.

Using tolerances at stage level is essential to the way the Project Board delegates and empowers the Project Manager, and to the exception management process.

Stage tolerances provide a defined area of discretion within which the Project Manager can be left to manage. Provided that the Project Manager's forecasts indicate that the stage will be completed within the time and cost parameters defined by the 'target box' (see Figure 3.1) there is no need for Project Board intervention. If forecasts suggest otherwise, however, the Project Manager must alert the Project Board to the 'exception'.

PRINCE2 also provides for tolerances applicable to quality, scope, benefits and risk.

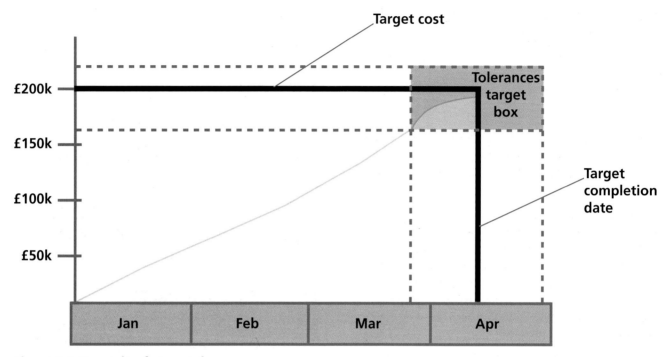

**Figure 3.1 Example of stage tolerances**

Besides being applied at stage level, tolerances are applied at the project level and may also be implemented at the level of individual Work Packages.

When an exception does occur, the Project Manager produces an Exception Report, which informs the Project Board members of the situation and outlines any different responses that may be appropriate, recommending a way forward if possible. Once the way forward has been agreed, the Project Manager is usually asked to produce an Exception Plan (an alternative may be to terminate the project).

Using the contract analogy again, escalation is necessary because the current stage contract is no longer viable and must be replaced as soon as possible by a new 'contract' in the form of an Exception Plan.

**Hints and tips**

Project Board members are often the first to spot an exception, such as a change in the wider programme or business environment that will have a significant impact on the project.

In this situation it is the responsibility of the Project Board to alert the Project Manager, even though the exception planning approach is otherwise the same.

If the exception relates to project-level tolerances, the Executive will need to escalate to corporate or programme management, because the project is forecast to exceed the authority given to the Project Board.

## 3.4 FACILITATE CROSS-FUNCTIONAL INTEGRATION

The project team is a temporary structure set up with specific responsibility for the project; it usually crosses the functional boundaries in the sponsoring organization(s). Project Board members must ensure that the project structure is recognized and respected in the host line structures, and that the Project Board's control is not undermined.

Projects are usually cross-functional: they often either cross the internal line function boundaries within an organization or involve entirely separate business entities. None of the individual organizations or functions sees the whole picture and each has its own objectives for the project. Various styles of 'matrix management' are used to reconcile these differing perspectives and PRINCE2 provides a well-proven model of roles and responsibilities for a temporary project organization (the Organization theme outlined in Chapter 2).

If the roles of project and line management relative to one another are not clear and agreed, there will be continual tension in the delivery process, with inevitable consequences on performance.

Whether problems such as this can be avoided usually depends on the extent to which PRINCE2, or the 'project culture', is embedded in the business. Some organizations are much more project-oriented than others, which means that the temporary project teams are recognized and given a degree of authority similar to (or even higher than) the permanent line functions within the business.

**Hints and tips**

OGC provides valuable guidance on embedding good management practices for projects, programmes and portfolios, notably in maturity models:

- PRINCE2 Maturity Model (P2MM)
- Portfolio, Programme and Project Management Maturity Model (P3M3™ for short).

Maturity models provide a proven means of improving performance by describing a logical, step-by-step progression to higher levels of organizational capability.

## 3.5 COMMIT RESOURCES

Project Board members are responsible for committing the resources necessary for the successful completion of the project.

When selecting Project Board members, it is an important criterion that, collectively, they should have the authority to deliver all the resources required for the success of the project.

The Project Manager is responsible for assembling the plans, and for identifying, communicating and agreeing the resource requirements with users and suppliers. The Project Board must then approve the plans for the work to begin.

It is important that Project Board members understand that, by approving a Project Plan or Stage Plan, they are endorsing it as a realistic plan and undertaking to commit the required resources. They cannot subsequently distance themselves from the plan content.

Resourcing issues are typically the ones most often escalated to Project Board members. Using their authority to resolve these issues generally provides the best opportunity for Project Board members to demonstrate senior management commitment and support for the Project Manager.

Many resourcing problems arise from competition for scarce resources and it is the Project Board with its wider perspective that is properly equipped to determine the business priorities.

## 3.6 ENSURE EFFECTIVE DECISION MAKING

Project Board members must ensure effective decision making.

The Project Board makes the key decisions in the project. Decision making is the means by which control is exerted, and PRINCE2 provides an optimized framework for this purpose.

### 3.6.1 Progress control

Once the project's initial direction has been agreed, the Project Board becomes primarily a progress control function. Progress is authorized by approving the Project Plan and Stage Plans. Approval should be given collectively by Project Board members to ensure that all stakeholder interests are understood and safeguarded.

Plans are approved and progress is assessed and reaffirmed at Project Board reviews, principally at stage boundaries. All Project Board reviews are based on the same simple agenda, as shown in the tinted box.

**Example of a typical Project Board agenda**

**1 Look back**
Review status in relation to the current Stage Plan (or Exception Plan)

**2 Look forward**
Preview the next Stage Plan (or Exception Plan)

**3 Assess overall project viability**
Consider the current status of the Business Case, Project Plan and issues/risks

**4 Make a decision**
Decide whether to give authorization to proceed by approving the next Stage Plan (or Exception Plan)

It can be seen that the reviews should always *focus on plans*, approving them and assessing progress in relation to them. This basic agenda is easily adapted for Project Board meetings at different points in the project's lifecycle, and quickly becomes a familiar and effective approach for decision making (see also Appendix C).

**Hints and tips**

*All* PRINCE2 reviews are designed to promote effective decision making:

- Checkpoints (working-level status reviews) enable the Project Manager to forecast whether progress will remain within tolerances
- Quality reviews are conducted to determine whether products are complete and fit for purpose
- Risk/issue reviews are conducted to determine responses to current risks and issues.

The Project Board agenda is organized in the way shown in the tinted box so that Project Board members are fully briefed on the current context of the project before stepping back from the detail (in agenda item 3) to assess the position in relation to the overall Project Plan and, most importantly, the Business Case.

The same approach and agenda apply equally well for Project Board reviews arising from exceptions.

**Hints and tips**

■ Project Board reviews are the key control milestones in PRINCE2 projects. Clearly, it is preferable for Project Board members to meet, face to face if possible, but, failing that, by using video or telephone conferences.

■ To ensure that senior managers are available (as their diaries are usually filled months ahead), the schedule of Project Board meetings should be agreed as soon as the pattern of stages is clear.

## 3.6.2 Risks, issues and changes

Decisions on minor risks, issues and changes can usually be delegated to the Project Manager. On complex projects, or if there is a high volume of change at the working level, the Project Board may appoint a Change Authority (a person or group) and delegate day-to-day risk/issue/change decisions on these matters.

However, some decisions (especially those that impact tolerances) must be reserved for the Project Board.

Who makes the decisions on particular categories of risks, issues and changes should be agreed when initiating the project and documented in the Project Initiation Documentation.

**Hints and tips**

■ If the project is part of a programme, it is essential that the processes for managing risks, issues and changes at the project level are integrated with those at the programme level.

■ Issues, risks and changes are all multi-dimensional, and different responses are often required at different levels (programme and project) and in different projects. The processes and tools used must accommodate this complexity.

■ There are different ways of categorizing risks (such as using the other five project variables: time, cost, scope, quality, benefits).

■ In an MSP programme, the arrangements for managing risks, issues and changes are detailed in programme documents such as the Risk and Issue Management Strategies.

There is an opportunity for discussing important risks, issues and/or changes at the Project Board reviews (agenda item 3). However, decisions on these are frequently made in an ad hoc manner (this is covered in Chapter 4).

## 3.6.3 Quality control

The Project Board contributes to quality control by approving:

■ The customer's quality expectations and acceptance criteria

■ A Quality Management Strategy (including key quality responsibilities)

■ Individual Product Descriptions for key project deliverables.

In other respects, Project Board members may or *may not* be the best-qualified people to participate in reviews of the project's specialist products. Nevertheless, Project Board members must ensure that the right people are involved in quality reviews, testing and any other quality-related responsibilities.

> **Hints and tips**
>
> The PRINCE2 manual, *Managing Successful Projects with PRINCE2* (TSO, 2009) provides a systematic technique for agreeing whether a document (or similar type of product) fulfils its requirements – the quality review. The technique can be applied to both management and specialist documentation – and is a tried and tested means of achieving agreement and facilitating approvals.

Senior Users need to know that people with the right practical experience are being involved at the working level and in quality inspections/reviews. Similarly, Senior Suppliers need to know that the right specialist technical expertise is being deployed. The focus of the Executive's concern is the quality of adherence to good project management practices and standards, including PRINCE2.

At the (stage boundary) Project Board reviews, the Project Manager will use information in the Quality Register to assure Project Board members that the agreed quality measures have been implemented and the right people have been involved.

### 3.6.4 Project Assurance

Another means by which Project Board members can ensure that decisions are well informed is by delegating Project Assurance responsibilities to people who are capable of monitoring the business, user and supplier interests at working level.

> **Hints and tips**
>
> ■ Project Assurance can be implemented in several ways, such as with independent, part-time or full-time assurance roles or with occasional, independent project health checks.
>
> ■ It is important to note that a delegated Project Assurance function has no accountability for the project, irrespective of the form it takes. The Project Board's accountability (for the project) and the Project Manager's responsibilities (for the stages) should not be compromised.
>
> ■ Programme-level functions, such as a design authority, programme office or quality assurance function can be valuable Project Assurance resources.

### 3.6.5 Informal decision making

Another consistent feature of PRINCE2 is that the formal control reviews represent incentives for the Project Manager and the team to get things agreed informally beforehand.

At Project Board reviews, particularly, there should be no surprises. There is rarely enough time at a Project Board review to examine plans in detail, but Project Board members nevertheless need to be confident about what they are signing up to.

It follows that the Project Manager will wish to discuss and resolve as many as possible of the important or contentious aspects of plans beforehand. It is important that Project Board members provide effective channels for this to happen, either directly or by using Project Assurance intermediaries.

## 3.7 SUPPORT THE PROJECT MANAGER

Project Board members must provide effective support for the Project Manager.

The Project Manager is the focus for the day-to-day management of the project work and this is often a busy and stressful role. The Project Board can remove some of the obstacles by demonstrating visible and sustained support for the Project Manager.

There are many ways of achieving this, such as:

- Ensuring that the Project Manager is sufficiently experienced and properly equipped for the scale of the project
- Emphasizing to all concerned that the Project Manager carries the Project Board's delegated authority during stages (and reinforcing this if it is challenged)
- Providing adequate Project Support resources so that the Project Manager can communicate and lead without getting overloaded by formalities and administrative work
- Listening carefully to the Project Manager's advice and considering what should be done to remove any obstacles; acting as a mentor, where appropriate
- Allowing time for planning (exerting pressure to get started on the deliverables is a common failing)
- Implementing supportive Project Assurance arrangements
- Being readily accessible for consultations, advice and guidance
- Responding promptly and constructively when issues are escalated
- Participating in all the formal Project Board reviews.

The Project Board should already be fulfilling other duties covered earlier:

- Using their influence to ensure that, wherever possible, the resources approved in plans are actually delivered
- Providing unified and consistent direction.

## 3.8 ENSURE EFFECTIVE COMMUNICATION

The Project Board must ensure that communication is timely and effective, both within the project and with key external stakeholders.

Project Board members are responsible for directing communication with stakeholders and acting as champions for the project. A large or complex project may involve a wide range of stakeholders, including members of the public. For this type of project, a formal Communication Management Strategy will be essential. On simple projects, the communications channels and messages may be agreed more informally.

Important aspects to consider are:

- Who are the audiences (internal and external) for project communication?
- How will they be affected by the project? Sometimes there will be unwelcome impacts, and communications must be particularly sensitive.
- What are the most appropriate channels in each case: personal contact, reports, email, newsletters, internet, press releases etc?
- What are the key messages? These must be:
  - Mutually consistent
  - Consistent with the Project Plan/Stage Plans.

■ When to communicate? A common problem is too much communication from different projects at the same time.

### Hints and tips

■ If the project is part of a programme, a wider Stakeholder Engagement Strategy will be approved by the Programme Board and communication will be directed, for the most part, at programme level.

■ Issuing numerous messages to stakeholders early on in a project can result in a perceived lack of momentum later on.

■ It is preferable to time communications to coincide with demonstrable progress.

■ As the handover to operational implementation approaches, stakeholders who have not been directly involved with the project may be anxious about its impact and are likely to need more information and reassurance.

■ Set realistic expectations – in particular, qualify budget estimates and target completion dates carefully according to the level of confidence in them. Quote ranges rather than absolute values until there is a good level of confidence.

■ Avoid bogus accuracy. Use 'round figures'.

### Hints and tips

■ Highlight Reports and End Stage Reports can also be used to inform line managers who are outside the immediate project team. This is sensible in that it avoids duplicating reports, but it can occasionally lead to confusing interventions by stakeholders outside the project management team.

■ It is important to communicate and reinforce the accountability of Project Board members (for directing project activity) and Project Managers (for managing it) in the wider organizational culture, so that managers outside the project management team understand who has authority and observe the correct channels for communicating with the project.

■ When the project is part of a programme, Project Board members are responsible for communicating effectively with the programme management sponsoring the project. To ensure that consistent and accurate messages are communicated, Project Board members often reserve the exclusive right to communicate at programme level.

Essential internal project communication is covered by the regular PRINCE2 disciplines – plans, Work Package definitions, Highlight Reports, End Stage Reports etc. Supplementary and 'social' communications such as newsletters are often useful but they should not obscure these basic information flows.

# Project Board activities

4

# 4 Project Board activities

The Project Board is primarily concerned with two PRINCE2 processes:

- Starting up a Project (a pre-project process carried out largely by the Project Executive and the Project Manager)
- Directing a Project (covering the five key types of Project Board review and the guidance on giving ad hoc direction).

This chapter summarizes the full guidance that is provided in the manual *Directing Successful Projects with PRINCE2* (TSO, 2009).

## 4.1 STARTING UP A PROJECT

The Project Board members and the Project Manager are appointed as a pre-project activity in the PRINCE2 process Starting up a Project. The Executive's appointment comes first, in the form of a project mandate approved by corporate or programme management.

During the Starting up a Project process (Figure 4.1), the Project Manager prepares a Project Brief, which outlines the key aspects of the proposed project, such as its scope and business justification. The Project Manager also prepares the Initiation Stage Plan, so that the detailed preparations for the project are brought under control as soon as possible.

> **Hints and tips**
>
> - Where a project is being managed as part of an MSP programme, the programme usually undertakes the activities in Starting up a Project. In these circumstances, the Project Board members are appointed by programme management and their remit is defined in a Project Brief agreed at programme level.
> - The purpose of the Initiation Stage Plan is to ensure that the project planning itself does not drift out of control. Without a plan, the discussions and negotiations involved in agreeing aspects such as project scope and approach can become protracted and costly.

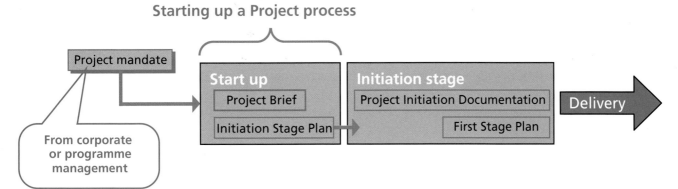

Figure 4.1 Starting up a Project

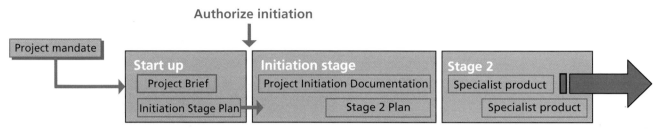

*Figure 4.2 Authorize initiation*

## 4.2 AUTHORIZE INITIATION

Authorizing initiation (Figure 4.2) is the first activity in the Directing a Project process. Its purpose is to decide whether it is worthwhile investing time and money in the development of a Business Case and detailed plans for the project. The Project Board decides whether to proceed by assessing the Project Brief prepared during Starting up a Project.

If the decision is made to proceed, the Project Board must also review and approve the Stage Plan for project initiation.

> **Hints and tips**
>
> ■ Allow enough time for a robust project initiation. Most project failures (by far) can be traced back to poor project initiation.
>
> ■ Initiation involves engaging key stakeholders (who are usually very busy senior managers) and gaining agreement on important aspects such as the project's detailed scope and approach.
>
> ■ Time is also required to ensure that the planned estimates, dependencies and schedules are realistic.

The model agenda for this Project Board review is included in Appendix C.

## 4.3 AUTHORIZE THE PROJECT

Authorizing the project (Figure 4.3) is the next activity in the Directing a Project process. Its purpose is to decide whether to commit to the project overall as a business investment. The decision is based on detailed Project Initiation Documentation (PID), developed from the Project Brief during the initiation stage.

If the PID is approved, it becomes the baseline for all forms of project control.

If the project is approved, the Project Board must also authorize a Stage Plan (see section 4.4) – with associated tolerances – to govern the activity of the next stage, when the work of developing the project's specialist products will begin.

The model agenda for this Project Board review is included in Appendix C.

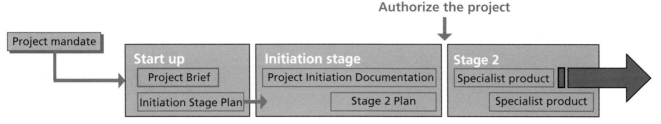

*Figure 4.3 Authorize the project*

**Hints and tips**

- There are six variables that need to be controlled and tolerances can be set for each (both at project and stage levels):
  - Time (for example, plus or minus a number of days)
  - Cost (for example, plus or minus a percentage of estimated cost)
  - Scope (for example: by providing a budget for small changes, if appropriate)
  - Quality (by expressing quality criteria in terms of a range of acceptable values rather than an absolute value)
  - Benefits (again, by expressing targets in terms of range values)
  - Risk (for example: if the expected value of a risk [the product of the likelihood of its occurring and the estimated cost/benefit of its impact] exceeds a certain value then the risk must be escalated as an exception).
- The PID includes a Business Case justifying the investment in the project. By approving the Business Case the Project Board accepts accountability for delivering it.
- The Business Case should include a benefits review strategy explaining how the project's benefits will be measured and reviewed both during and after the project.

## 4.4 AUTHORIZE A STAGE OR EXCEPTION PLAN

After initiation, the project progresses as a series of one or more delivery stages, during which the products of the project are created.

The Project Board authorizes a Stage Plan at each stage boundary (Figure 4.4).

However, even in a well-managed project, it has to be accepted that projects are inherently risky and things will not always go to plan. PRINCE2 accommodates this by including the requirement for the Project Manager to raise 'exceptions' when, for whatever reason, forecasts suggest that a stage is unlikely to be completed within agreed tolerances. When Exception Reports are raised, Project Board will often request that the Project Manager prepares an Exception Plan to account for the impact of the exception.

In these circumstances, the Project Board authorizes the Exception Plan, which becomes a replacement for the current Stage Plan (Figure 4.5).

The model agenda for this Project Board review is included in Appendix C.

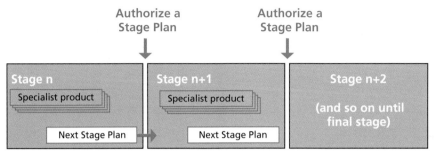

*Figure 4.4 Authorize a Stage Plan*

**Hints and tips**

■ Resolving an exception can often be relatively simple, for example by making a minor adjustment to the scope, by increasing the budget or by an acceptable delay. In these circumstances, the full formality of an Exception Plan and a Project Board review is unnecessary. Nevertheless, any changes involved must be recorded and approved by the Project Board members.

■ Regardless of the cause, escalating an exception to the Project Board is evidence of good project management, and Project Board members should respond accordingly.

## 4.5 GIVE AD HOC DIRECTION

Giving ad hoc direction (Figure 4.6) is an important aspect of Directing a Project providing opportunities to support the Project Manager and to communicate and delegate effectively (consistent with the duties and behaviours described in Chapter 3). Project Board members can provide direction individually or collectively.

The purpose of this activity is to ensure that there is a consistent and thorough mutual understanding between the Project Board, the Project Manager and Project Assurance throughout the project.

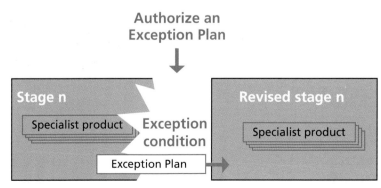

*Figure 4.5 Authorize an Exception Plan*

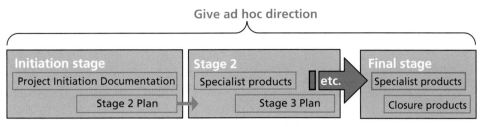

**Figure 4.6 Give ad hoc direction**

**Hints and tips**

When giving ad hoc direction individually, Project Board members should be mindful of other members' interests and views, consistent with the duty to provide unified direction. They should consult and keep each other informed.

## 4.6 AUTHORIZE PROJECT CLOSURE

Authorizing project closure (Figure 4.7) is the last Project Board activity. Its purpose is to confirm that the project has been concluded in an orderly manner, whether successfully or prematurely, before the project team is disbanded.

The Project Board needs to be assured that there has been a complete handover and acceptance of the project's products by the functions responsible for using and maintaining them, that the arrangements and ownership of any follow-on action have been agreed, that measures are in place to realize the benefits from the project, and that the participating organizations will exploit any lessons learned.

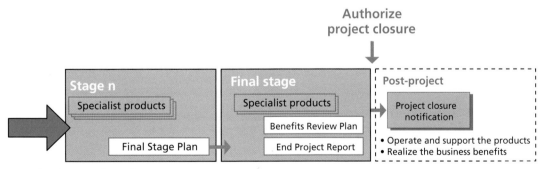

**Figure 4.7 Authorize project closure**

## 4.7 REVIEWING BENEFITS

Project benefits are usually realized after project closure (Figure 4.8). However, PRINCE2 also includes process guidance for situations in which benefits are achieved during the project's lifetime.

The Business Case for a project should include a benefits review strategy, which is reviewed and approved by the Project Board (see section 4.3).

When benefits are achieved during a project, they should be reviewed by the Project Board at the stage boundaries and confirmed at project closure.

For benefits achieved after project closure, PRINCE2 provides for the Project Board to review and approve a Benefits Review Plan in the course of confirming project closure. This plan sets out the arrangements for a benefits review to be held at a suitable date in the future.

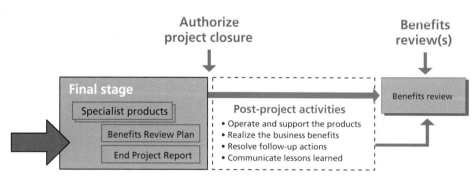

*Figure 4.8  Reviewing benefits*

# Programmes and portfolios

5

# 5 Programmes and portfolios

Chapter 1 introduced the concepts of programmes and portfolios – structures within which projects are frequently organized. This chapter discusses good practices in programme and portfolio management and how they relate to senior managers in Project Board roles.

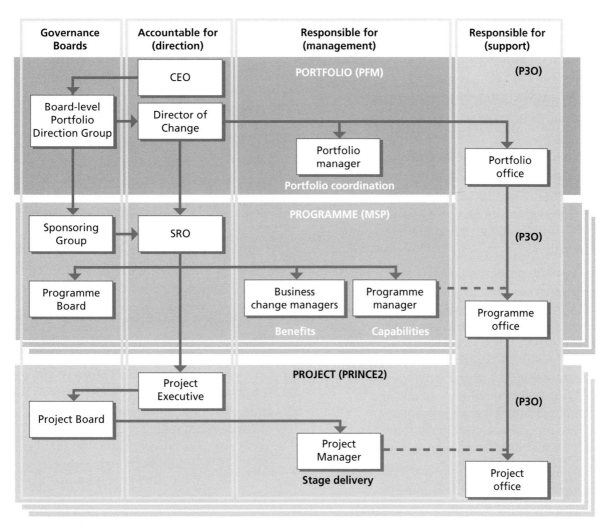

*Figure 5.1 Functions and roles in the OGC best-practice guidance*

## 5.1 OVERVIEW OF PROGRAMME AND PORTFOLIO ROLES

Figure 5.1 shows a simplified illustration of the key roles in directing projects, programmes and the portfolio – not all the functions are included. The chain of individual accountability and the various management responsibilities are shown in the vertical 'swim-lanes' of the diagram. The Governance Boards shown are equally crucial as a means of achieving unified, cross-functional direction and decision making.

## 5.2 THE PROGRAMME MANAGEMENT (MSP) CONTEXT

### 5.2.1 'Vision-led' business change programmes

Projects are very often inter-related, sometimes because the projects are of a similar specialist nature (IT, construction etc.) and share the same specialist resources.

Another key way projects can be linked is where an organization is aiming to introduce a large-scale change in order to gain strategic business benefits. In this type of programme, even though they are inter-related, the nature of the individual projects may be quite different. OGC's programme management guidance, *Managing Successful Programmes* (TSO, 2007), is primarily designed to manage this type of strategic business change programme. In this context, programme management has two objectives, requiring different management skill-sets:

- To introduce new capabilities into the business (programme and project delivery)
- To realize the benefits of the business change (operational 'business as usual', after the change).

**Hints and tips**

In practice, the structures at the three levels often overlap. For instance, an individual senior manager might be a Management Board member, a member of the Sponsoring Group for a particular programme and a Project Board member for a business-critical project.

So that the framework can readily be scaled, tailored and integrated to the needs of a specific organization, this basic picture needs to be clarified with some rules:

- Roles may be full- or (more often) part-time (depending on factors such as scale and strategic importance)
- One person may take on more than one role within a programme. Typically a programme's Senior Responsible Owner (SRO) may also be the Executive for a major project in the programme. However, some roles cannot be combined – for example, a Project Manager cannot have a Project Board role on the same project
- One person may have roles on more than one project or programme (or even portfolio). For example, one person may serve as a Project Board member on several different projects. This helps to improve the integration between programmes and projects
- In some cases, a role may be divided between more than one person, and again, this is constrained by rules; for example, the SRO, the Project Executive and the Project Manager roles should never be shared.

**Hints and tips**

Vision-led programmes may comprise many projects and take years to implement. MSP advises that this type of programme should be divided into a series of 'tranches' – that is, groups of projects that contribute towards key 'step-changes' during the programme. This helps sustain the focus on delivering the new capabilities and realizing the proposed benefits as the programme evolves.

## 5.2.2 Integrating the MSP and PRINCE2 themes

The structure of MSP is very similar to that of PRINCE2, and each has a set of themes. MSP and PRINCE2 are fully compatible: combining them largely involves integrating the respective themes, in particular, the Organization theme.

Table 5.1 maps the relationship between the MSP governance themes and the PRINCE2 themes.

As shown in Table 5.1, the MSP governance themes often reflect the themes in PRINCE2, so many of the disciplines can be consolidated at the programme level to reduce duplication at project level and improve consistency.

- Project initiation overheads are reduced by work completed at programme level (such as Business Cases and strategies for risk, change and quality management).
- Project documentation follows standards set at the programme level, improving consistency.
- Consistent standards result in better communication and information management. They also facilitate the use of software support tools where necessary (reporting 'dashboards', risk, issue and change control support tools etc.).
- Some functions should logically be shared across projects (examples are configuration management, continuous improvement, the evaluation of lessons learned, performance analysis).

**Table 5.1 Mapping MSP and PRINCE2 themes for integration**

| MSP governance theme | Related PRINCE2 theme(s) |
| --- | --- |
| Organization | Organization |
| Vision | (Affects solution designs and thus Plans) |
| Leadership and stakeholder engagement | Organization |
| Benefits realization management | Business Case; Progress |
| Blueprint design and delivery | (Affects solution designs and thus Plans) |
| Planning and control | Plans; Progress |
| Business Case | Business Case; Progress |
| Risks and issue management | Risk; Change |
| Quality management | Quality |

### Hints and tips

To achieve integration with PRINCE2, use the management strategies described in the MSP governance themes (and listed below) to define consolidated approaches across the programme, so that less definition is required at project level:

- Benefits Management Strategy
- Information Management Strategy
- Issue Resolution Strategy
- Monitoring and Control Strategy
- Quality Management Strategy
- Resource Management Strategy
- Stakeholder Engagement Strategy.

Note that these efficiencies apply to any type of programme – not just 'vision-led' programmes – so these aspects of MSP are of value regardless of the programme type.

MSP's governance themes for vision and blueprint design and delivery are more specific to 'vision-led' programmes. They describe work that is carried out exclusively at the programme level.

### 5.2.3 Integrating the MSP and PRINCE2 organizations

The PRINCE2 project organization is explained in Chapter 2 (and illustrated in Figure 2.1). Figure 5.2 shows the programme management organization recommended by MSP. The key roles are expanded below.

#### *Sponsoring Group*

This is the group of senior managers responsible for the investment decision, for interpreting the strategic direction of the business and for ensuring the ongoing alignment of the programme to that strategic direction.

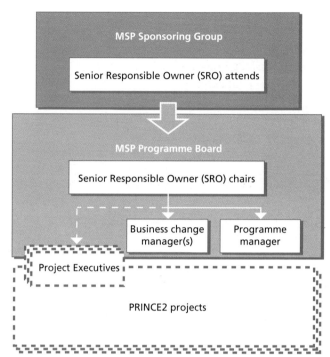

**Figure 5.2 MSP governance and roles**

The Sponsoring Group is the driving force behind the programme and appoints the SRO.

### Hints and tips

Members of the Sponsoring Group for a programme may also be members of the overall Portfolio Direction Group recommended in PfM (see section 5.3). They should, in any case, remain closely aligned to the strategic direction defined by that Group.

#### *Senior Responsible Owner*

This is the single individual with overall responsibility for ensuring that the programme meets its objectives and delivers the expected benefits. The SRO must have adequate authority in the business to make things happen.

The SRO for a programme may additionally take on the Project Executive role for key projects within the programme.

Some organizations appoint SROs to direct large free-standing projects. In this case, the SRO simply takes on the PRINCE2 Project Executive role.

Exceptionally, an SRO may choose to delegate some responsibilities to a full-time specialist programme director but they should never delegate decision making on key decision points for the programme. The SRO retains ultimate responsibility for the success of the programme/project.

### Business change manager(s)

This is the role responsible for benefits management, from identification through to realization. The aim is to ensure that the new capabilities delivered by the projects in the programme are properly implemented and embedded in the sponsoring organization(s). Thus business change managers often have long-term line management responsibilities for realizing benefits.

Usually, there will be more than one business change manager for a programme, to manage impacts in different parts of the organization (or in different organizations). It is sometimes advisable to establish a change team to support the business change managers and contribute specialist business change skills.

There is a direct relationship between the programme-level role of the business change managers and the Project Board role of Senior Users, so business change managers may also act as Senior Users at project level.

Depending on the nature of the project and the expertise of the person concerned, a business change manager might also act as the Project Executive.

### Programme manager

This is the role responsible for the set-up, management and delivery of the programme. It is important that the person undertaking this role has the necessary programme and project management experience and expertise.

Programme managers may also act as Project Board members. However, this is not always appropriate. The programme manager may not have the required line authority to supervise the people acting as Senior Users and Senior Suppliers (who normally do have senior line management positions).

Also, a programme manager may not have the authority to commit key resources, which is a crucial requirement for the Senior User and Senior Supplier roles.

## Programme Board

The Programme Board is chaired by the SRO and its members include the programme manager and the business change manager(s). The role of the Programme Board is to support the SRO and supply the necessary cross-functional governance forum for key decisions.

As in PRINCE2 (with Project Boards), the Programme Board is responsible for programme assurance, building confidence in the sponsoring organization(s) by ensuring that all aspects of the programme are being managed properly.

### Hints and tips

MSP advises that the Project Executives for the major projects in the programme might also be included as members of the Programme Board, to ensure strategic alignment and promote integration.

Programmes vary considerably in terms of scale and complexity, and MSP suggests that a number of 'other governance roles' should be considered and established, if necessary. These may or may not be included as members of the Programme Board:

- A design authority to provide strategic-level governance and specialist advice (such as in the IT or construction context)
- A programme accountant (or finance manager) to manage compliance with corporate accounting procedures and support for Business Case development
- A benefits realization manager to support the business change managers (who often also carry line responsibilities) with specialist expertise in this field

- A procurement manager – many programmes include a high proportion of procurement activity
- A risk manager with specialist expertise in this field.

### Hints and tips

- Another role often found at this level is that of quality manager, responsible for quality assurance and continuous improvement in the programme. The role can be valuable for analysing performance metrics and lessons learned, supporting standards and processes and carrying out audits and health checks. Alternatively, quality management may be a function of the sponsoring organization.
- When some or all of these appointments are made at programme level, there is a valuable opportunity for them to support the Project Board and provide additional project-level assurance. Note, however, that the roles are included to provide focused advice and guidance; the Project Board remains accountable for the project overall.

## Programme office

The programme office is the information hub and standards custodian for the programme and its delivery objectives. Programme offices take different forms depending on the programmes and organizations that they support.

## 5.3 THE PORTFOLIO MANAGEMENT CONTEXT

### 5.3.1 The business change portfolio

MSP and PRINCE2 address the management of programmes of business change and the individual projects involved. Portfolio management is about selecting and delivering those changes that contribute most to the organization's strategic objectives by selecting the right programmes and projects from competing ideas and proposals.

Unlike programmes and projects, which close once their objectives have been realized, a portfolio of change is a permanent feature of the organization concerned (whether or not it is actively managed).

Portfolio management must be integral to the organization's permanent governance, aligned to the strategic planning function. Decisions about the content of the portfolio, or any changes, must be taken by the Management Board (or the leadership team of the business unit concerned). The purpose of portfolio management is to provide evidence-based mechanisms that inform the decisions at this level.

The portfolio contains the current and future programmes and projects that have been prioritized, scheduled and endorsed by the Management Board or leadership team concerned.

Each programme/project is linked to one or more of the organization's strategic objectives and has its resources, dependencies and benefits identified. The aim is to select the right business changes (according to the overall business strategy) and give them the right relative priorities.

The OGC PfM guidance is expressed as principles, cycles and practices that are expanded in terms of real-life examples of their application. The principles address:

- The need for Management Board-level sponsorship of portfolio management
- The need to integrate PfM as a function of the organization's permanent governance

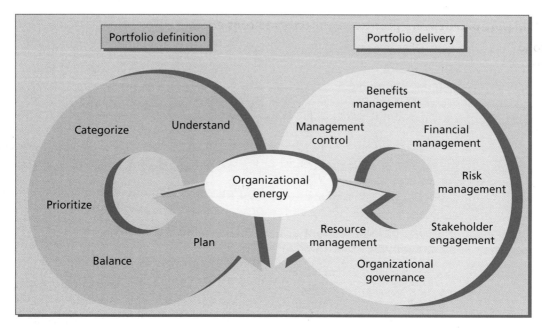

**Figure 5.3 Portfolio management cycles**

- The need to integrate PfM with strategic planning
- The need for integrated support and administrative processes for the programmes and projects within the portfolio with a PfM support function at the top level (see P3O®, Appendix A)
- The challenge of engaging, inspiring and motivating the whole organization towards the changes involved.

## 5.3.2 Implementing PfM

PfM practices are divided into two simultaneous cycles of activity (shown in Figure 5.3):

- The **Portfolio Definition Cycle**: closely aligned with strategic planning, these practices involve understanding, categorizing, prioritizing, balancing and planning the portfolio. These are strategic-level practices: while they influence activity at programme and project level, the activities do not overlap with programme-level MSP governance. This cycle is led by a Management Board-level Portfolio Direction Group
- The **Portfolio Delivery Cycle**: the practices required to ensure that the portfolio objectives are realized through the various programmes and projects (Table 5.2). Table 5.2 outlines some of the benefits and factors for consideration. This cycle is led by the Portfolio Progress Group (not shown in Figure 5.1).

**Table 5.2  PfM portfolio delivery practices and factors to consider**

| PfM portfolio delivery practice | Factors to consider |
| --- | --- |
| Management control | PfM requires that there should be a standard 'business change lifecycle' for each programme – that is, each programme should pass through a standard set of milestones (gates) for management reporting and assurance purposes. The OGC Gateway review process is one example of the way this can be done and is also fully compatible with the programme and project delivery framework described in this guide (see Appendix A). |
| Benefits management | PfM aims to ensure that the benefits and benefits realization strategies of individual MSP programmes continue to reflect the overall strategic objectives of the portfolio. The PfM disciplines promote consistency at programme level, such as in documentation and measurement, providing additional expertise to increase accuracy and avoid double-counting of benefits. |
| Financial management | Finance department processes and accounting cycles can be very disruptive for programmes of change. PfM focuses on integrating financial processes/reporting to best overall effect for the organization. The outcome should be clearer, more efficient and more consistent funding and financial rules at programme level. |
| Risk management | PfM aims to create consistency in the approach to risk management across the programmes; to establish the support infrastructure required (with appropriate rules for risk promotion and demotion); and to control the overall level of risk exposure for the organization. |
| Stakeholder engagement | Working closely with the corporate communication team, the PfM aim is to implement a centrally managed and consistent approach to stakeholder engagement and communication within which the programme-level strategies can operate. Useful aspects include access to funding from any corporate communication budgets that might apply and systematic attention given to feedback from key stakeholders. |
| Organizational governance | This PfM practice addresses the strategic level integration of change management within the existing governance arrangements of the organization. It only affects MSP governance at programme level in the sense that the importance of change programmes will be more effectively recognized and supported by the organization as a whole. |
| Resource management | The PfM practice enables the high-level resource forecasts from programme-level Business Cases to be used as input to strategic resource plans, and then refined as the programmes progress through management control gates. Resourcing can then be adjusted and any conflicts resolved in line with portfolio priorities. |

### 5.3.3 Integrating the PfM roles in the organization

Standard portfolio management roles are not rigidly prescribed in the OGC guidance but an example structure is provided and some clear recommendations are given, for example:

- A Management Board member is a champion for portfolio management (such as a director of business change, or 'transformation director')
- Some form of portfolio manager role exists to coordinate portfolio delivery on a day-to-day basis
- A portfolio office exists to collate information about portfolio progress (in 'dashboard' form) and inform senior management decisions about business change.

Portfolio management is necessarily collaborative. Change initiatives have repercussions across an organization, so senior managers involved in portfolio management will need to ensure that there are systematic and appropriate contacts with key business functions, such as:

- Finance
- IT
- Procurement/commercial
- Strategic planning (annual and longer-term plans)
- Business architecture planning (for example, for blueprints, future operating models)
- Performance measurement (for example, for balanced scorecards)
- Programme and project management divisions
- Human resources
- Estate and property services
- Centres of excellence (or equivalent functions), e.g. expert training and consultancy support for highly specialized skills.

The key PfM roles are described below, with examples of how they may overlap with the senior management roles in MSP and PRINCE2.

#### Business change director

The business change director is the Management Board member who owns the vision for the portfolio, providing clear leadership and direction through its life. The role requires strong leadership and management skills coupled with the authority to champion the delivery of complex implementations.

The business change director needs to develop and maintain robust relationships with all parts of the business as well as with the programmes and projects, to ensure that Management Board members and their teams are supportive of PfM.

**Hints and tips**

- The business change director may also be a member of the Sponsoring Group for individual programmes and may act as SRO.
- For a business-critical project, the business change director might even take on the role of the Project Executive.

#### Portfolio manager

The portfolio manager's role is to coordinate the successful delivery of the Portfolio Delivery Strategy on a day-to-day basis.

The portfolio manager leads on implementing all key practices, ensuring that the Portfolio Progress Group and Portfolio Direction Group receive the right information to make informed decisions.

While the role may or may not be directly responsible for changes in the portfolio, he or she will lead the definition and delivery of the overall portfolio and be the first point of contact for new change proposals. The individual must have substantial experience with strategic, programme and project management.

**Hints and tips**

- The portfolio manager may be a member of the Sponsoring Group for individual programmes and may act as the SRO for a programme or the Executive on a project.
- However, for the SRO or Project Executive roles, it is important to ensure that the person concerned has the necessary authority in the organization (relative to the other members of the Programme or Project Board concerned). If not, there is the possibility that unified direction may be undermined.

# Troubleshooting 6

# 6  Troubleshooting

This chapter outlines some of the problems that can occur during delivery of a project and how senior managers can diagnose or avoid them using the framework of OGC best practices.

More detailed advice can be found in:

- *Managing Successful Projects with PRINCE2* (TSO, 2009) (Appendix D), which contains a detailed, process-related health checklist that can be used by Project Assurance
- *Managing Successful Programmes* (TSO, 2007) (Appendix D), which also contains comprehensive guidance on programme-level health checks.

## 6.1  PROJECT PERFORMANCE

Performance issues on individual projects are usually related to inadequate attention to one or more of the PRINCE2 themes. This section introduces some of the ways that senior managers, in this case Project Board members, can spot and avoid the typical symptoms of project failure.

### 6.1.1  Business Case and benefits

The purpose of the Business Case theme is to keep the focus on the project's contribution to achieving worthwhile benefits for the business. Table 6.1 provides a list of preventive measures that the Project Board can take to resolve Business Case problems.

**Table 6.1  Resolving project Business Case problems**

| Problem | Project Board preventive measures |
| --- | --- |
| Uncertainty over business purposes or objectives | ■ Check that the key business, user and supplier stakeholders and resource providers are represented on the Project Board<br>■ Assess whether there are too many members on the Project Board (ideally no more than five)<br>■ If necessary, explain the purpose of Advisory Board(s) and introduce them<br>■ Make sure there is an unambiguous project justification with clearly defined, agreed and communicated benefits<br>■ Consider undertaking a feasibility or scoping study to clarify purposes and objectives<br>■ Consider terminating the project |
| Different interpretations of purposes and/or objectives | ■ Make sure the project justification is agreed by all key stakeholder interests (business, user and supplier) and communicated effectively |

*Table continues*

**Table 6.1 Resolving project Business Case problems** *continued*

| Problem | Project Board preventive measures |
| --- | --- |
| Lack of confidence in benefits | ■ Make sure that the benefits are agreed as realistic<br><br>■ Make sure that the Senior User(s) own and are committed to realizing the agreed benefits<br><br>■ Define the benefits in ways that can be measured (even if by proxy measures) as this helps to focus on what needs to be done to realize the benefits<br><br>■ Consider a 'proof of concept' exercise early in the project (or as a separate project) to validate the benefits<br><br>■ Seek evidence (lessons learned) from earlier, similar projects to validate the potential benefits |
| Lack of confidence in ability to deliver within cost and/or timescale targets | ■ Make sure that all key estimates, assumptions and dependencies are included in plans<br><br>■ Get assurance that all key estimates, assumptions and dependencies are realistic<br><br>■ Get assurance that user and supplier stakeholders understand and agree the requirements in sufficient detail<br><br>■ Make sure that ongoing supplier assurance is in place to confirm the extent of progress and risks<br><br>■ Make sure that ongoing user assurance is in place to confirm user obligations are being met and requirements are being fulfilled<br><br>■ Discourage changes to requirements unless they have strong business justification<br><br>■ Make sure that plans address the higher-risk aspects of the work as early as possible to build confidence |
| Lack of confidence in selected project approach | ■ Make sure that other options for the project approach have been adequately considered<br><br>■ Get assurance that all user and supplier stakeholders fully understand and agree the project approach<br><br>■ Extend the consultation period. Many projects start too early, before all stakeholders have been fully consulted and genuine buy-in for the project approach is achieved<br><br>■ Consider conducting a feasibility study, developing prototypes or running pilots |
| Costs escalating | ■ Get assurance that costs are under adequate control (Senior Supplier)<br><br>■ Initiate a project audit or health check. Has this project issue been properly recorded and assessed for impact/resolution? Has exception management been invoked where necessary?<br><br>■ Instruct the Project Manager to prepare a Lessons Report examining the reasons the original estimates were incorrect and the likely impact, and recommending new measures to improve estimation or control costs<br><br>■ Make sure that the Business Case is still viable, otherwise consider terminating the project |
| Lack of confidence that benefits will be realized | ■ Make sure that there is sufficient focus on benefits realization (Senior User)<br><br>■ Make sure that the project is still viable, otherwise consider terminating the project |

## 6.1.2 Organization

The purpose of the Organization theme is to make sure that the right people are involved in decision making and project management, and that their roles and responsibilities are defined and understood. Table 6.2 provides a list of preventive measures that the Project Board can take to resolve project organization problems.

**Table 6.2 Resolving project organization problems**

| Problem | Project Board preventive measures |
|---|---|
| Key personnel unwilling to serve on the Project Board | ■ This is a serious risk – there is a demonstrable lack of commitment to the project. Make sure that the project is consistent with/important to strategic plans. If not, consider terminating it. Otherwise, escalate the issue to programme or portfolio level |
| Uncertainty over roles and responsibilities | ■ Make sure that the roles and responsibilities in the project organization are clearly defined, understood and agreed with all participants<br>■ Make sure that the participants have the necessary authority and access to resources, as well as the skills and training to do their jobs<br>■ Make sure that the project organization is understood and recognized by the sponsoring organization(s) |
| Insufficient or ineffective communication | ■ Make sure that the Project Manager is leading and communicating<br>■ Establish a Communication Management Strategy with clear responsibilities and messages<br>■ Make sure that the Project Manager is not overloaded with administrative activities and that there is enough Project Support resource |
| Supplier resources not available | ■ If the resource requirements differ from those estimated in plans, assess whether inaccurate estimates represent a serious risk to the project's viability<br>■ If the requirements are consistent with plans but the timing has changed, assess whether the problem could have been anticipated/resolved earlier<br>■ If the requirements and timing are consistent with plans, assess whether there is a lack of supplier commitment |
| User resources not available | ■ If the resource requirements differ from those estimated in plans, assess whether inaccurate estimates represent a serious risk to the project's viability<br>■ If the requirements are consistent with plans but the timing has changed, assess whether the problem could have been anticipated/resolved earlier<br>■ If the requirements and timing are consistent with plans, assess whether there is a lack of user commitment |
| Team unsure of project direction | ■ Make sure there is unified direction at Project Board level<br>■ Get assurance that Project Board direction is being interpreted accurately and effectively by the Project Manager<br>■ Make sure that managers outside the project organization are not intervening or contributing to the confusion over direction |

### 6.1.3 Quality

The purpose of the Quality theme is, firstly, to make sure that the scope of the project is clearly defined and understood and, secondly, to ensure that the organization's expectations for product quality are realized.

During the start-up and initiation of projects, careful consideration should be given to defining project scope appropriately in relation to any other linked projects or activities.

The scope and quality aspects in PRINCE2 place considerable emphasis on Product Descriptions. Table 6.3 provides a list of preventive measures that the Project Board can take to resolve project quality problems.

**Table 6.3 Resolving quality problems**

| Problem | Project Board preventive measures |
| --- | --- |
| Confusion over project scope | ■ Make sure that the Product Descriptions, product breakdown structure (for scoping the project's products) and project approach are sufficiently detailed and agreed by users and suppliers |
| Overly complex scope with many work-streams and stakeholders | ■ Consider the advantages of managing the work as a number of linked projects within a programme structure |
| Simple scope, short timescale, single work-stream and what appears to be a heavy project management overhead | ■ Determine whether this really is a project. Consider managing the task as a Work Package. Perhaps it should be bundled with other similar (but unrelated) tasks in a 'support service'<br>■ If the work is closely linked to other parallel tasks, consider whether the scope boundaries of the various projects might be rearranged to better effect |
| Dissatisfaction with product quality | ■ Make sure that Product Descriptions are sufficiently detailed and properly agreed<br>■ Look for evidence that the quality controls specified in Product Descriptions are being applied<br>■ Make sure instances of quality failure are being properly recorded (as 'off-specifications') and dealt with. If not, this is a sign that project management is not sufficiently rigorous<br>■ Get assurance that the right people (users and suppliers) are responsible for carrying out the quality controls and that they have the appropriate training<br>■ Encourage cross-functional quality controls wherever possible (the product supplier and user review and/or test the product together instead of in a series of isolated reviews, which tend to introduce disputes) |

## 6.1.4 Plans

The purpose of the Plans theme is to make sure that there is a robust framework of baseline plans to provide the focus for project communication and control. Table 6.4 provides a list of preventive measures that the Project Board can take to resolve problems with Project or Stage Plans.

**Table 6.4 Resolving problems with plans**

| Problem | Project Board preventive measures |
|---------|-----------------------------------|
| Poor plans | ■ Allow enough time for planning |
| | ■ Make sure that the Project Manager works closely with those who will generate the products when producing the plans. If this is not possible, recognize that there is a substantial risk |
| | ■ Make sure that there is adequate assurance during planning, particularly on the supplier side |
| | ■ Be available for consultation during the planning process. Challenge the evolving plans |
| | ■ Obtain specialist planning support, for example from programme level |
| | ■ Manage expectations – qualify timescale and cost estimates according to the level of confidence there is. Use 'range' estimates rather than 'point' estimates until there is a good measure of confidence in the plans |
| | ■ Make sure that plans are complete – including Product Descriptions, estimates and assumptions, dependencies, risks and countermeasures |
| | ■ Make sure that the project objectives are clear and not obscured by detail. The schedule approved by the Project Board should be expressed at a high level, with the key delivery milestones highlighted |
| | ■ At the same time, seek assurance that there is confidence in the detail – that the Work Packages and Team Plans are realistic |
| | ■ Make sure that all Project Board members are fully committed to the plans before authorizing further progress |
| | ■ Accept ownership of a plan once it has been approved |

### 6.1.5 Risk

The management of risks should be a constant factor in decision making throughout the project. The purpose of the Risk theme is to ensure that there is a systematic approach to identifying and dealing with threats and opportunities. Table 6.5 provides a list of preventive measures that the Project Board can take to resolve problems with risk management.

**Table 6.5 Resolving risk management problems**

| Problem | Project Board preventive measures |
|---|---|
| The sponsoring business does not want to hear about risks | ■ Ultimately, it is always the sponsor's Business Case that is at risk, regardless of contractual provisions. Clarify the business impact of risks in discussions |
| Problems not anticipated | ■ Look for evidence that the Project Manager is regularly and systematically reviewing risks and that the right people are involved in the reviews<br>■ Obtain specialist risk management support, for example from programme level<br>■ Define 'early warning indicators' and monitor them |
| Missed opportunities | ■ Look for evidence that the risk reviews consider potential improvements to the project approach and plans |
| Risk responses (mitigation, fallback etc.) not prepared or updated | ■ Look for evidence that risk management is proactive and does not simply involve a periodic check of the Risk Register<br>■ Obtain specialist risk management support, for example from programme level |

## 6.1.6 Change

The purpose of the Change theme is to ensure that there is a systematic response to any issues, change requests or instances of quality failure that may arise, so that all work on the project is properly authorized and accounted for. Table 6.6 provides a list of preventive measures that the Project Board can take to resolve change problems.

**Table 6.6 Resolving change problems**

| Problem | Project Board preventive measures |
|---|---|
| Issues overlooked or allowed to drift | ■ Look for evidence that the Project Manager is regularly and systematically reviewing issues and changes, and that the right people are involved in the reviews |
| | ■ Look for evidence that owners are identified for all issues, changes and quality failures |
| | ■ Make sure that the rules and arrangements for escalating issues, changes and quality failures are clear, and that they are properly communicated |
| Evidence of activity that is not specified in plans | ■ Check the potential for 'scope creep'. Make sure that all activity has been properly authorized, either in a plan or in response to a documented issue/change |
| | ■ Check whether there is unauthorized or informally approved activity. All work should be authorized, either in an approved plan or as an agreed response to a recorded risk/issue. If not, this is usually evidence of poor project management (planning, control or both) and should be investigated quickly |
| | ■ Make sure that work is not being directed from outside the project management organization |
| Unforeseen high volume of change requests | ■ Check whether there are potential issues with the quality of requirements definition. Get assurance that requirements and the project approach have been formally agreed |

### 6.1.7 Progress

The purpose of the progress theme is to ensure that the project proceeds in line with its original business purposes and under effective business control.

Progress control covers the approval of plans, monitoring, reporting, escalation and the management of exceptions. Table 6.7 provides a list of preventive measures that the Project Board can take to resolve progress issues.

**Table 6.7 Resolving problems with progress**

| Problem | Project Board preventive measures |
| --- | --- |
| Unexpected delays or cost overruns | ■ Make sure that the management stage structure for the project is sensible |
| | ■ Look for assurances that there is an appropriate level of confidence in Project and Stage Plans |
| | ■ Make sure that there is a clear understanding of tolerances for time and cost between the Project Board and the Project Manager |
| | ■ Look for evidence that the Project Manager is regularly and systematically monitoring expenditure and achievement, and forecasting performance versus tolerances |
| | ■ Monitor the Highlight Reports for consistency and accuracy – challenge and/or follow up where appropriate (Project Managers often complain about the amount of time consumed in reporting and the lack of senior management response) |
| | ■ Look for evidence that individual delays/cost overruns have been recorded, at least as project issues. Otherwise, it is a sign that project management is not sufficiently rigorous |
| | ■ Make sure that the Project Manager reports all exceptions and that, whenever possible, the Project Board responds constructively. |
| Unexpected bad news at Project Board meetings | ■ Make sure the Project Manager understands that there should be no surprises at Project Board meetings |
| | ■ Explain that the Project Board expects early warning of any significant progress issues and that exceptions must be reported immediately |
| | ■ Check that individual issues are being recorded and managed as they arise – and not being allowed to accumulate. If this is not the case, it is a sign that project management is not sufficiently rigorous |
| | ■ Explain that Project Board members expect the opportunity to discuss and informally approve any potentially contentious aspect of plans ahead of meetings |
| | ■ Make sure that Project Board members are accessible to the Project Manager, especially at stage boundaries when the need for consultations is most likely |
| Questionable Business Case viability | ■ Make sure that the focus remains on business objectives – not simply time, cost and quality |
| | ■ Ensure that the Project Manager and the key stakeholders are alert to factors that might influence the viability of the Business Case |

| Problem | Project Board preventive measures |
|---|---|
| Project direction or momentum uncertain | ■ Establish the Project Board's authority and accountability for the project |
| | ■ Make sure that this is recognized and supported within the sponsoring organization(s) |
| | ■ Schedule Project Board meetings well in advance and make sure all members attend |
| | ■ Establish and maintain unified direction |
| | ■ Make sure that the focus of Project Board meetings is on reviewing and approving progress based on plans. (If Project Board meetings simply focus on current issues rather than plans, it is a sign that the project is drifting out of control) |
| | ■ If necessary, consider terminating the project |
| Too many meetings | ■ Make sure that meetings are properly focused. Project Board progress reviews should focus on the plans and the Business Case. Issues and risks that are important in that context need to be discussed, but avoid getting caught up in too much talk and not enough decision making |
| | ■ The Project Manager should be empowered to manage the everyday risk, issues and quality-related reviews, escalating only where necessary |

## 6.2 PERFORMANCE OF THE OVERALL ORGANIZATION

Performance at the level of the individual project has been shown to depend, in large measure, on the capability and maturity of the sponsoring organization. Organizations with higher levels of maturity will experience more consistency, predictability and success in the conduct of their projects and programmes, as well as improvements in efficiency.

This is reflected in the growing use of 'maturity models' that offer organizations a step-by-step approach to improving the way they manage development in areas such as IT – and business change generally. Organizations undertaking capability/maturity initiatives frequently report an excellent return on their investment (see Appendix A for an outline of the OGC maturity models P2MM and P3M3).

Many of the organizational improvements required for higher levels of maturity are embedded in the OGC programme- and portfolio-level guidance. Table 6.8 addresses some of the difficulties that occur when these wider, organizational disciplines are not in place.

**Table 6.8 Resolving problems with the organization's overall performance**

| Problem | Senior management preventive measures |
|---|---|
| Performance is inconsistent from project to project | ■ Make sure project and programme management processes and methods are defined, accessible and properly communicated to all concerned (not just Project Managers). The implication is that there must be a corporate, portfolio or programme-level function responsible for achieving this |
| | ■ Make sure that there is adequate training and support available for the processes and tools to be used. Again, the implication is that there will be resources available for this – typically in a corporate centre of excellence, a portfolio office or a programme office |
| | ■ Make sure that there is adequate quality assurance and that audits and health checks are carried out to check that there is an acceptable level of process conformance |
| | ■ Make sure that the processes and tools are relevant and appropriate. Provide feedback mechanisms (such as lessons learned). Analyse and act upon the feedback so that there is genuine continuous improvement |
| Senior managers find it difficult to understand the extent of business change going on, or how the various changes inter-relate | ■ The organization's portfolio is not adequately defined and/or communicated |
| | ■ Make sure that effective PfM disciplines are introduced and that the information is communicated properly |
| Senior managers find it difficult to see where the real problems are and what needs attention | ■ Make sure that the reporting, escalation and information management regimes from projects through programmes to the portfolio level are consistent and effective |
| | ■ Assess whether there is too much information and too many different types of report |
| Too much change and not enough resources | ■ The portfolio may be unrealistic, insufficiently prioritized or unbalanced. Make sure that appropriate PfM Portfolio Definition practices are introduced |
| Different parts of the business are not aware of each other's plans | ■ Assess whether Portfolio Definition is inadequate, poorly communicated and/or not well enough integrated with business operations (business as usual). Integrate the PfM practices into the normal business governance of the organization |
| | ■ Aim for a consistent approach to configuration management (including ownership responsibilities, processes and tools) across projects and programmes, where possible |
| Projects and programmes always seem to be 'overtaken by events' | ■ Make sure that portfolio management is a fully integrated component of the organization's normal business governance |
| | ■ Make sure that stakeholder engagement and communication are effective at programme level |

| Problem | Senior management preventive measures |
|---|---|
| The business is not learning from its mistakes (or successes). Lessons Reports are produced but nobody ever does anything about them | ■ Make sure that the process of seeking and recording lessons learned at project level is translated in to 'organizational learning' and continuous improvement at programme level and above<br><br>■ Check whether programme/portfolio-level functions such as quality assurance, process management or continuous improvement are systematically assessing lessons learned in case changes or improvements need to be made to processes, methods and standards |
| All project estimates and assumptions are recorded and actual performance is measured, but the accuracy of estimation does not seem to be improving | ■ Estimates, assumptions and actual performance data should always be recorded for effective progress control at project level. Make sure that, wherever possible, this information is used to refine estimation models and guidance |

# Appendix A:
# Other OGC guidance

# Appendix A: Other OGC guidance

## A.1 PORTFOLIO, PROGRAMME AND PROJECT OFFICE (P3O)

PfM, MSP and PRINCE2 describe the accountabilities and responsibilities for delivering change in portfolios, programmes and projects, respectively. Collectively, they provide a framework for decision making at the three levels of business change governance.

The role of P3O is to provide an appropriate decision-enabling and delivery support infrastructure for business change in the organization. PfM, MSP and PRINCE2 outline the requirements for support at each level in the infrastructure, but it is a P3O model that provides for the vertical integration of the support services (as illustrated in Figure A.1).

The P3O infrastructure can take many different forms:

■ It may be a single, permanent office with a variety of possible titles, such as portfolio office, strategic or business planning unit, centre of excellence, corporate or enterprise programme office

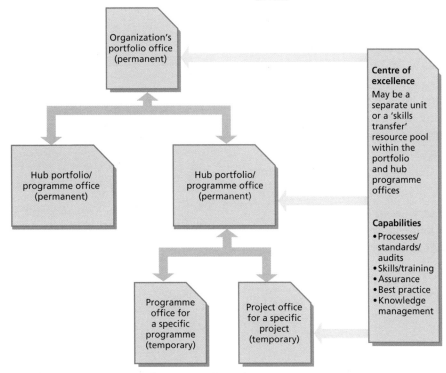

*Figure A.1 Example of a P3O structure of support functions*

- It may take the form of a linked set of offices providing a mix of central and localized services, such as a permanent portfolio office with temporary programme and project offices.

The profile of the services in a particular organization depends on factors such as the number of programmes and projects concerned, the size of the resource pool, and the structure and nature of the business itself. Figure A.1 shows one possible arrangement for a large organization.

**Hints and tips**

Large supplier-type organizations may define and manage separate 'hub' portfolios for each customer sector (or each large customer) in a similar structure to that shown in Figure A.1.

In a small organization, however, the entire P3O resource may consist of just one or two people providing administrative and limited specialist support.

In an immature or new P3O, the services and functions offered are limited to data gathering, reflecting the lack of competency of individuals, whereas in a mature P3O, individuals will possess the competencies to offer a wide range of services/functions, challenging and using the data gathered.

The functions and services in P3O should be tailored to individual programmes and projects, but within a consistent underlying performance culture.

## A.2 OGC'S GATEWAY REVIEW

The OGC's Gateway review process was introduced in Chapter 3 as an example of a peer review and in Chapter 5 as one example of the type of 'business change' lifecycle that is required for portfolio-level management control to operate effectively.

The Gateway review process involves examining programmes and projects at key decision points in their lifecycle. It looks ahead to provide assurance that they can progress successfully to the next gate. Gateway 0 is designed as a programme-level gate that can be repeated throughout the programme. Gateways 1–4 are considered to be project-level gates and relate particularly to procurement projects. Gateway 5 is also a repeating review; it is concerned with benefits realization and operational effectiveness.

**Hints and tips**

In practice, similar or additional gateways can be implemented either at programme or project level and tailored to key decision points, without so much focus on procurement. There is a considerable amount of generic gateway review guidance that would still be applicable and valuable, such as guidance to review teams on 'delivery confidence'.

The six decision points, or gateways, in the programme/project lifecycle are outlined in Table A.1. There is also a 'starting gate' for policy-related programmes and projects.

**Table A.1 Gateways in the programme/project lifecycle**

| Gateway | Description |
|---|---|
| Starting gate | This review applies at the early stages of the policy-to-delivery lifecycle and is undertaken before a programme or project has formally started. Its purpose is to assess the link between good policy making and operational delivery. |
| Gateway 0: strategic assessment | Designed as a programme-level gate, this can be repeated at key points throughout a programme – from inception to exit strategy. The gate consists of an examination of the direction and planned outcomes of the programme together with the progress of its constituent projects. |
| Gateway 1: business justification | The first project review comes after the Strategic Business Case has been prepared and before the development proposal is approved. The focus is on the project's business justification. |
| Gateway 2: delivery strategy | This review investigates the Outline Business Case and the delivery strategy before any formal approaches are made to prospective suppliers or delivery partners. The review may be repeated in long or complex procurement situations. |
| Gateway 3: investment decision | This review investigates the full Business Case and the governance arrangements for the investment decision. The review takes place before a work order is in place with a supplier and funding and resources committed.<br><br>A project will normally go through a single OGC Gateway Review 3. However, in some circumstances, it may be necessary for a project to repeat the OGC Gateway Review 3, such as in construction projects. |
| Gateway 4: readiness for service | This review focuses on the readiness of the organization to go live with the necessary business changes, and the arrangements for management of the operational services and/or new facilities. |
| Gateway 5: operations review and benefits realization | This review confirms that the desired benefits of the project or programme are being achieved, and the business changes are operating smoothly. The review is repeated at regular intervals during the lifetime of the new service/facility. |

## A.3 RELEVANT OGC MATURITY MODELS

Maturity models are management tools designed to help organizations implement effective processes for a given discipline – in this case, portfolio, programme and project management. They are developed on the basis that organizations cannot move from zero capability to optimum capability instantaneously. Instead, organizations progress along a journey of maturity.

PRINCE2, MSP and PfM describe a framework of best practices for managing projects and business change generally. The maturity models provide valuable help to embed these disciplines in the culture of the organization.

Maturity models describe a number of maturity levels, the lowest being 'initial' – characterized by 'chaotic, ad hoc' processes and success achieved only by 'heroic efforts'. The highest level is characterized by continuous improvement and process optimization.

OGC is developing a maturity model in support of the best-practice frameworks outlined in this guide:

■ Portfolio, Programme and Project Management Maturity Model (P3M3) (www.ogc.gov.uk/documents/p3m3.pdf)

Useful guidance is also published in the linked publication:

■ *Improving Project Performance Using the PRINCE2 Maturity Model (P2MM)* (TSO, 2007)

# Appendix B:
# About PRINCE2

B

# Appendix B: About PRINCE2

This appendix summarizes the key characteristics of PRINCE2: its principles, themes and processes. It also outlines the benefits of adopting PRINCE2 as a corporate standard.

## B.1   PRINCE2 PRINCIPLES

The following principles represent essential PRINCE2 practice: if a project does not implement them all, it is not using PRINCE2.

- The project must have continued business justification.
- The project team must actively learn from experience throughout.
- The project must have a defined structure of roles and responsibilities based on the PRINCE2 model.
- The project must be managed as a series of stages (a minimum of two).
- 'Management by exception': tolerances must be defined to establish the limits of delegated authority within the project management structures.
- 'Product focus': scope and quality requirements must be defined in relation to products.
- The implementation of PRINCE2 must be tailored to suit the project's environment, size, complexity, importance, capability and risk.

## B.2   PRINCE2 THEMES

Themes are those aspects of project management that need to be:

- Addressed continually throughout the project
- Implemented in line with the PRINCE2 guidance so that the overall project management framework is properly integrated.

**Table B.1  The PRINCE2 themes**

| Theme | Scope |
| --- | --- |
| Business Case | Defining and regularly reviewing the business justification (answers the question: Why?) |
| Organization | Defining and observing the roles and responsibilities in the project organization structure (Who?). This guide is aimed at the senior roles in the structure – that is, the Project Board members |
| Quality | Defining scope; defining and achieving quality requirements (What?) |
| Plans | Product-based planning for the project, the stages and the teams (How? How Much? When?) |
| Risk | Identifying, communicating and managing threats and opportunities throughout the project (What if?) |
| Change | Deciding and implementing the project's response to issues, changes and quality problems throughout the project (What's the impact? How do we respond?) |
| Progress | Assessing project status and taking decisions on project progress (Where are we now? Where are we going? Should we carry on?) |

Table B.1 summarizes the scope of the PRINCE2 themes.

## B.3 THE PRINCE2 PROCESSES

The requirements of the various themes are integrated in the process model, which describes the step-by-step activities that need to be done by the different members of the project management team as the project progresses.

The processes are listed in Table B.2 and the points at which they are carried out are illustrated in Figure B.1.

This guide focuses on the two processes carried out by the Project Board members – the most senior managers in the project organization. These are Starting up a Project and Directing a Project.

**Table B.2 The PRINCE2 processes**

| Process | Abbreviation | Performed by |
|---|---|---|
| Starting up a Project | SU | Project Board and Project Manager |
| Directing a Project | DP | Project Board |
| Initiating a Project | IP | Project Manager |
| Controlling a Stage | CS | Project Manager |
| Managing Product Delivery | MP | Team Manager |
| Managing a Stage Boundary | SB | Project Manager |
| Closing a Project | CP | Project Manager |

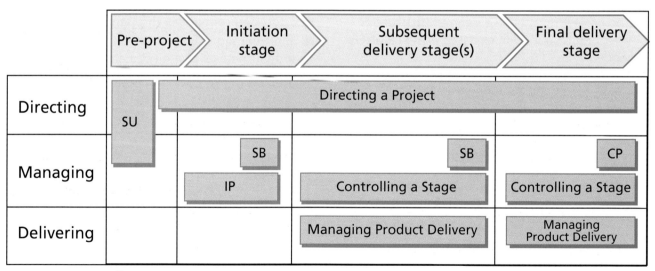

Key
SU = Starting up a Project
IP = Initiating a Project
SB = Managing a Stage Boundary
CP = Closing a Project

*Figure B.1 The PRINCE2 process model*

**Hints and tips**

Three levels of management (Project Board, Project Manager and Team Manager) may seem like too much for a small project but, in PRINCE2, some roles can be combined and performed by one person.

For small projects the same person will often perform the roles of Project Manager and Team Manager.

However, two levels of management will always be required – senior managers (the Project Board) to direct the effort and commit the resources and Project Managers to provide day-to-day control.

## B.4 BENEFITS OF ADOPTING PRINCE2

PRINCE2 is widely adopted as a corporate standard because:

- It embodies proven best practice and governance for project management
- It can be applied to any type of project and can easily be implemented alongside specialist, industry-specific models ('engineering models' or 'development lifecycles')
- It is widely understood, providing a common vocabulary for all project participants and promoting effective communication
- It is fully compatible with OGC's *Managing Successful Programmes* (TSO, 2007) and consistent with a range of other relevant best practices, including advice on portfolio management
- It clarifies project responsibilities, so that participants understand each other's roles and needs. There is a defined structure for accountability, delegation, authority and communication

- The focus on the project's products clarifies (for all parties) what the project will deliver, why, when, by whom and for whom
- Its plans are carefully designed to meet the needs of the different levels in the project team, improving communication and control
- It employs 'management by exception', so that there is efficient and economic use of management time
- It ensures that participants retain a focus on the business objectives, rather than simply seeing the completion of the project as an end in itself
- It defines a thorough but economical structure of reports
- It ensures that stakeholders are properly represented in planning and decision making
- Adopting PRINCE2 promotes consistency in project work across an organization, providing a basis for continuous improvement
- It provides opportunities to re-use project assets such as documentation
- It facilitates staff mobility and reduces the impact of personnel changes/handovers
- It is an invaluable diagnostic tool, facilitating project audits, health checks and troubleshooting
- There are scores of accredited training and consultancy organizations (ATOs and ACOs) operating worldwide, which can supply expert support for PRINCE2 projects or for organizations planning to adopt PRINCE2 as a corporate standard.

# Appendix C:
# Project Board
# agendas

# Appendix C: Project Board agendas

The following generic Project Board meeting agenda was introduced in Chapter 4.

> **Example of a typical Project Board agenda**
>
> **1 Look back**
> Review status in relation to the current Stage Plan (or Exception Plan)
>
> **2 Look forward**
> Preview the next Stage (or Exception) Plan
>
> **3 Assess overall project viability**
> Consider the current status of the Business Case, Project Plan and issues/risks
>
> **4 Make a decision**
> Decide whether to give authorization to proceed by approving the next Stage Plan (or Exception Plan).

This basic agenda can be applied at every key decision point in the project, as shown in the following examples.

## C.1 AUTHORIZE INITIATION

> **Suggested Project Board agenda for authorizing initiation**
>
> **1 Look back**
> Review the background to the project and the Project Brief
>
> **2 Look forward**
> Preview the Initiation Stage Plan
>
> **3 Assess overall project viability**
> Review the outline Business Case and key issues/ risks
>
> **4 Make a decision**
> Authorize the initiation stage to commence (by approving the Initiation Stage Plan and Project Brief).

## C.2 AUTHORIZE THE PROJECT

Suggested Project Board agenda for authorizing the project

**1 Look back**
Review the End Stage Report from the initiation stage

**2 Look forward**
Review the Project Initiation Documentation

**3 Assess overall project viability**
Review the Business Case and key issues/risks

**4 Make a decision**
Authorize the project (by approving the Project Initiation Documentation), or

Request amendments to the Project Initiation Documentation, or

Reject the project.

## C.3 AUTHORIZE A STAGE OR EXCEPTION PLAN

Suggested Project Board agenda for authorizing a Stage or Exception Plan

**1 Look back**
Review status in relation to the current Stage Plan (or Exception Plan)

**2 Look forward**
Review the next Stage Plan or Exception Plan

**3 Assess overall project viability**
Consider the current status of the Business Case, Project Plan and issues/risks

**4 Make a decision**
Authorize the stage to proceed by approving the next Stage Plan (or Exception Plan), or

Request premature closure if the project is no longer viable or desirable.

## C.4 AUTHORIZE PROJECT CLOSURE

**Suggested agenda for authorizing project closure**

**1 Look back**
Review the End Project Report

Review the Lessons Report and actions

**2 Look forward**
Review the Benefits Review Plan

Approve the follow-on action recommendations

**3 Assess overall project viability**
Confirm the final costs and expected benefits in the Business Case

**4 Make a decision**
Authorize project closure by approving a project closure notification.

## C.5 RE-AFFIRM APPROVAL FOR A STAGE PLAN

Project Board members sometimes wish to meet during a stage – particularly a long stage – in order to stay in touch with the work and build confidence in progress. Provided that the principle of management by exception is not undermined, this is perfectly consistent with PRINCE2 and the Project Board agenda can, again, be tailored quite simply as shown in the box below.

**Example of a typical Project Board agenda**

**1 Look back**
Review status in relation to the current Stage Plan

**2 Look forward**
Preview the Stage Plan activities scheduled up to the next Project Board meeting

**3 Assess overall project viability**
Consider the current status of the Business Case, Project Plan and issues/risks

**4 Make a decision**
Decide whether to re-affirm approval of the current Stage Plan.

# Appendix D:
# Product Descriptions

An indication of any specialist skills/

# Appendix D: Product Descriptions

Product Descriptions are essential to PRINCE2's principle of 'product focus' and the linked techniques of product-based planning. They are the means by which an unambiguous understanding and agreement are achieved on the precise scope and quality requirements for a project (see section 6.1.3 for advice on product quality).

A full Product Description consists of the following:

- Identifier and title
  Unique for a product (or type of product)

- Purpose
  What is it for? Who will use it?

- Composition
  A list of the parts of the product

- Derivation
  What are the source products from which this one is derived? (Example: a design is derived from a requirements specification)

- Format and presentation
  Characteristics such as whether a report should take the form of a document, a slide presentation or an email

- Development skills required
  An indication of any specialist skills/ competencies required to develop the product or an indication of the area that will supply the development resources

- Quality criteria
  What quality attributes and/or measurements must the finished product have? What standards must be met?

- Quality tolerance
  Details of any range in the quality criteria within which the product would be acceptable

- Quality method
  How will the product be checked (examples: inspection, review, piloting, testing)?

- Quality skills
  An indication of any specialist skills/ competencies required to check the product or an indication of which area will supply the resources for checks

- Quality responsibilities
  Who will produce the product? Who will review it? Who will approve it?

The manual *Managing Successful Projects with PRINCE2* (TSO, 2009) contains abbreviated Product Description outlines for all required management products, and the manual *Directing Successful Projects with PRINCE2* (TSO, 2009) contains the ones typically used by Project Board members. These PRINCE2 Product Descriptions are not templates with a prescriptive content; they are designed to be used as the starting point for developing project-specific Product Descriptions.

The Product Description outline for Project Initiation Documentation is shown here as an example.

## PROJECT INITIATION DOCUMENTATION

### Purpose

The purpose of the Project Initiation Documentation is to define the project, in order to form the basis for its management and an assessment of its overall success. The Project Initiation Documentation gives the direction and scope of the project and (along with the Stage Plan) forms the 'contract' between the Project Manager and the Project Board.

The three primary uses of the Project Initiation Documentation are to:

- Ensure that the project has a sound basis before asking the Project Board to make any major commitment to the project
- Act as a base document against which the Project Board and Project Manager can assess progress, issues and ongoing viability questions
- Provide a single source of reference about the project so that people joining the 'temporary organization' can quickly and easily find out what the project is about, and how it is being managed.

The Project Initiation Documentation is a living product in that it should always reflect the current status, plans and controls of the project. Its component products will need to be updated and re-baselined, as necessary, at the end of each stage, to reflect the current status of its constituent parts.

The version of the Project Initiation Documentation that was used to gain authorization for the project is preserved as the basis against which performance will later be assessed when closing the project.

### Composition

There follows a contents list for the Project Initiation Documentation. Note that the first two (project definition and project approach) are extracted from the Project Brief.

- **Project definition** Explaining what the project needs to achieve. It should include:
  - Background
  - Project objectives and desired outcomes
  - Project scope and exclusions
  - Constraints and assumptions
  - The user(s) and any other known interested parties
  - Interfaces

- **Project approach** To define the choice of solution that will be used in the project to deliver the business option selected from the Business Case, taking into consideration the operational environment into which the solution must fit
- **Business Case** Describing the justification for the project based on estimated costs, risks and benefits
- **Project management team structure** A chart showing who will be involved with the project
- **Role descriptions** For the project management team and any other key resources
- **Quality Management Strategy** Describing the quality techniques and standards to be applied, and the responsibilities for achieving the required quality levels
- **Configuration Management Strategy** Describing how and by whom the project's products will be controlled and protected
- **Risk Management Strategy** Describing the specific risk management techniques and standards to be applied, and the responsibilities

for achieving an effective risk management procedure

- **Communication Management Strategy** To define the parties interested in the project and the means and frequency of communication between them and the project
- **Project Plan** Describing how and when the project's objectives are to be achieved, by showing the major products, activities and resources required on the project. It provides a baseline against which to monitor the project's progress stage by stage
- **Project controls** Summarizing the project-level controls such as stage boundaries, agreed tolerances, monitoring and reporting
- **Tailoring of PRINCE2** A summary of how PRINCE2 will be tailored for the project.

## Format and presentation

The Project Initiation Documentation could be:

- A single document
- An index for a collection of documents
- A document with cross-references to a number of other documents
- A collection of information in a project management tool.

## Quality criteria

- The Project Initiation Documentation correctly represents the project.
- It shows a viable, achievable project that is in line with corporate strategy or overall programme needs.
- The project management team structure is complete, with names and titles. All the roles have been considered and are backed up by agreed role descriptions. The relationships and lines of authority are clear. If necessary, the project management team structure says to whom the Project Board reports.
- It clearly shows a control, reporting and direction regime that can be implemented, appropriate to the scale, risk and importance of the project to corporate or programme management.
- The controls cover the needs of the Project Board, Project Manager and Team Managers and satisfy any delegated assurance requirements.
- It is clear who will administer each control.
- The project objectives, approach and strategies are consistent with the organization's corporate social responsibility directive, and the project controls are adequate to ensure that the project remains compliant with such a directive.
- Consideration has been given to the format of the Project Initiation Documentation. For small projects a single document is appropriate. For large projects it is more appropriate for the Project Initiation Documentation to be a collection of standalone documents. The volatility of each element of the Project Initiation Documentation should be used to assess whether it should be standalone, e.g. elements that are likely to change frequently are best separated out.

# Glossary

# Glossary

### approval

The formal confirmation that a product is complete and meets its requirements (less any concessions) as defined by its Product Description.

### assumption

A statement that is taken as being true for the purposes of planning, but which could change later. An assumption is made where some facts are not yet known or decided, and is usually reserved for matters of such significance that, if they change or turn out not to be true, there will need to be considerable replanning.

### assurance

All the systematic actions necessary to provide confidence that the target (system, process, organization, programme, project, outcome, benefit, capability, product output, deliverable) is appropriate. Appropriateness might be defined subjectively or objectively in different circumstances. The implication is that assurance will have a level of independence from that which is being assured. *See also* Project Assurance and quality assurance.

### authority

The right to allocate resources and make decisions (applies to project, stage and team levels).

### authorization

The point at which an authority is granted.

### baseline

Reference levels against which an entity is monitored and controlled.

### benefit

The measurable improvement resulting from an outcome perceived as an advantage by one or more stakeholders.

### benefits management

The identification, definition, tracking, realization and optimization of benefits within and beyond a programme.

### benefits realization manager

An optional role within an organization that is responsible for maintaining a permanent centre of expertise in benefits realization within the organization, providing an objective challenge of benefits, dependencies, measures, targets and a programme's approach to benefits realization.

### benefits realization plan

A complete view of all the benefit profiles in the form of a schedule.

### Benefits Review Plan

A plan that defines how and when a measurement of the achievement of the project's benefits can be made. If the project is being managed within a programme, this information may be created and maintained at the programme level.

### blueprint

A model of a business or organization, its working practices and processes, the information it requires and the technology that will be needed to deliver the capability described in the vision statement.

### business as usual

The way a business normally achieves its objectives.

### Business Case

The justification for an organizational activity (project), which typically contains costs, benefits, risks and timescales, and against which continuing viability is tested.

### Business Case management

The manner in which a programme's rationale, objectives, benefits and risks are balanced against the financial investment, and how this balance is maintained, adjusted and assessed during the programme.

### business change lifecycle

Any organizational process or framework that helps to guide the delivery of programmes and projects using a collection of repeatable processes and decision points.

### business change manager

The role responsible for benefits management, from identification through to realization and ensuring the implementation and embedding of the new capabilities delivered by the projects. Typically allocated to more than one individual and also known as a change agent.

### capability

A service, function or operation that enables an organization to exploit opportunities.

### centre of excellence

A corporate coordinating function for portfolios, programmes and projects providing standards, consistency of methods and processes, knowledge management, assurance and training.

### Change Authority

A person or group to which the Project Board may delegate responsibility for the consideration of requests for change or off-specifications. The Change Authority may be given a change budget and can approve changes within that budget.

### change budget

The money allocated to the Change Authority available to be spent on authorized requests for change.

### change control

The procedure that ensures that all changes that may affect the project's agreed objectives are identified, assessed and either approved, rejected or deferred.

### change team

A group of specialists appointed to support a business change manager in the business change management aspects of benefits realization.

### checkpoint

A team-level, time-driven review of progress.

## closure notification

Advice from the Project Board to inform all stakeholders and the host sites that the project resources can be disbanded and support services, such as space, equipment and access, demobilized. It should indicate a closure date for costs to be charged to the project.

## Communication Management Strategy

A description of the means and frequency of communication between the project and the project's stakeholders.

## configuration management

Technical and administrative activities concerned with the creation, maintenance and controlled change of configuration throughout the life of a product.

## corporate or programme standards

These are over-arching standards that the project must adhere to. They will influence the four project strategies (Communication Management Strategy, Configuration Management Strategy, Quality Management Strategy and Risk Management Strategy) and the project controls.

## corporate portfolio

The totality of the change initiatives within an organization; it may comprise a number of programmes, standalone projects and other initiatives that achieve congruence of change.

## dashboard

A technique used by management to represent vast amounts of decision-support information at an amalgamated level using tabular and graphic aids such as graphs and traffic lights.

## dependencies (plan)

The relationship between products or activities. For example, the development of Product C cannot start until Products A and B have been completed. Dependencies can be internal or external.

Internal dependencies are those under the control of the Project Manager. External dependencies are those outside the control of the Project Manager – for example, the delivery of a product required by this project from another project.

## embedding

(PRINCE2) What an organization needs to do to adopt PRINCE2 as its corporate project management method. See also, in contrast, tailoring, which defines what a project needs to do to apply the method to a specific project environment.

## exception

A situation where it can be forecast that there will be a deviation beyond the tolerance levels agreed between Project Manager and Project Board (or between Project Board and corporate or programme management).

## Exception Plan

This is a plan that often follows an Exception Report. For a Stage Plan exception, it covers the period from the present to the end of the current stage. If the exception were at project level, the Project Plan would be replaced.

## Exception Report

A description of the exception situation, its impact, options, recommendation and impact of the recommendation. This report is prepared by the Project Manager for the Project Board.

### Executive

The single individual with overall responsibility for ensuring that a project meets its objectives and delivers the projected benefits. This individual should ensure that the project maintains its business focus, that it has clear authority, and that the work, including risks, is actively managed. The Executive is the chair of the Project Board. He or she represents the customer and is responsible for the Business Case.

### follow-on action recommendations

Recommended actions related to unfinished work, ongoing issues and risks, and any other activities needed to take a product to the next phase of its life. These are summarized and included in the End Stage Report (for phased handover) and End Project Report.

### governance (corporate)

The ongoing activity of maintaining a sound system of internal control by which the directors and officers of an organization ensure that effective management systems, including financial monitoring and control systems, have been put in place to protect assets, earning capacity and the reputation of the organization.

### governance (project)

Those areas of corporate governance that are specifically related to project activities. Effective governance of project management ensures that an organization's project portfolio is aligned to the organization's objectives, is delivered efficiently and is sustainable.

### handover

The transfer of ownership of a set of products to the respective user(s). The set of products is known as a release. There may be more than one handover in the life of a project (phased delivery). The final handover takes place in the Closing a Project process.

### Highlight Report

A time-driven report from the Project Manager to the Project Board on stage progress.

### impact (of risk)

The result of a particular threat or opportunity actually occurring, or the anticipation of such a result.

### initiation stage

The period from when the Project Board authorizes initiation to when they authorize the project (or decide not to go ahead with the project). The detailed planning and establishment of the project management infrastructure is covered by the Initiating a Project process.

### issue

A relevant event that has happened, was not planned, and requires management action. It can be any concern, query, request for change, suggestion or off-specification raised during a project. Project issues can be about anything to do with the project.

### leadership

The ability to direct, influence and motivate others towards a better outcome.

## Lessons Report

A report that documents any lessons that can be usefully applied to other projects. The purpose of the report is to provoke action so that the positive lessons from a project become embedded in the organization's way of working and that the organization is able to avoid the negative lessons on future projects.

## management product

A product that will be required as part of managing the project, and establishing and maintaining quality (for example, Highlight Report, End Stage Report etc.). The management products stay constant, whatever the type of project, and can be used as described, or with any relevant modifications, for all projects. There are three types of management product: baselines, records and reports.

## management stage

The section of a project that the Project Manager is managing on behalf of the Project Board at any one time, at the end of which the Project Board will wish to review progress to date, the state of the Project Plan, the Business Case and risks, and the next Stage Plan in order to decide whether to continue with the project.

## milestone

A significant event in a plan's schedule, such as completion of key Work Packages, a technical stage or a management stage.

## off-specification

Something that should be provided by the project, but currently is not (or is forecast not to be) provided. This might be a missing product or a product not meeting its specifications. It is one type of issue.

## opportunity

An uncertain event that could have a favourable impact on objectives or benefits.

## outcome

The result of change, normally affecting real-world behaviour and/or circumstances; the manifestation of part or all of the new state conceived in a programme's blueprint.

## output

A specialist product that is handed over to a user(s). Note that management products are not outputs but are created solely for the purpose of managing the project.

## P3M3

OGC's Portfolio, Programme and Project Management Maturity Model.

## performance targets

A plan's goals for time, cost, quality, scope, benefits and risk.

## plan

A detailed proposal for doing or achieving something which specifies the what, when, how and by whom. In PRINCE2 there are only the following types of plan: Project Plan, Stage Plan, Team Plan, Exception Plan and Benefits Review Plan.

## portfolio

The totality of an organization's investment (or segment thereof) in the changes required to achieve its strategic objectives.

## portfolio management

A coordinated collection of strategic processes and decisions that together enable the most effective balance of organizational change and business as usual.

## product

An input or output, whether tangible or intangible, that can be described in advance, created and tested. PRINCE2 has two types of products – management products and specialist products.

## product breakdown structure

A hierarchy of all the products to be produced during a plan.

## Product Description

A description of a product's purpose, composition, derivation and quality criteria. It is produced at planning time, as soon as possible after the need for the product is identified.

## product flow diagram

A diagram showing the sequence of production and interdependencies of the products listed in a product breakdown structure.

## product-based planning

A technique leading to a comprehensive plan based on the creation and delivery of required outputs. The technique considers prerequisite products, quality requirements and the dependencies between products.

## programme

A temporary flexible organization structure created to coordinate, direct and oversee the implementation of a set of related projects and activities in order to deliver outcomes and benefits related to the organization's strategic objectives. A programme is likely to have a life that spans several years.

## programme assurance

Independent assessment and confirmation that the programme as a whole or any of its aspects are on track, applying relevant practices and procedures, and that the projects, activities and business rationale remain aligned to the programme's objectives.

## Programme Board

A group that is established to support a Senior Responsible Owner to deliver a programme.

## programme management

The coordinated organization, direction and implementation of a dossier of projects and transformation activities (i.e. the programme) to achieve outcomes and realize benefits of strategic importance.

## programme manager

The role responsible for the set up, management and delivery of a programme; typically allocated to a single individual.

## programme office

The function providing the information hub and standards custodian for a programme and its delivery objectives; could provide support for more than one programme.

## programme organization

How a programme will be managed throughout its lifecycle; the roles and responsibilities of individuals involved in the programme; and personnel management or human resources arrangements. Also known as programme organization structure.

## project

A temporary organization that is created for the purpose of delivering one or more business products according to an agreed Business Case.

## project approach

A description of the way in which the work of the project is to be approached. For example, are we building a product from scratch or buying in a product that already exists?

## Project Assurance

The Project Board's responsibilities to assure itself that the project is being conducted correctly. The Project Board members each have a specific area of focus for Project Assurance, namely business assurance for the Executive, user assurance for the Senior User(s), and supplier assurance for the Senior Supplier(s).

## Project Brief

Statement that describes the purpose, cost, time and performance requirements, and constraints for a project. It is created pre-project during the Starting up a Project process and is used during the Initiating a Project process to create the Project Initiation Documentation and its components. It is superseded by the Project Initiation Documentation and not maintained.

## Project Initiation Documentation

A logical set of documents that brings together the key information needed to start the project on a sound basis and that conveys the information to all concerned with the project.

## project lifecycle

The period from the start up of a project to the acceptance of the final project product. Model project lifecycles can be constructed for specific types of project, ideally including Product Descriptions for the specialist products required in the course of that type of project.

## project management

The planning, delegating, monitoring and control of all aspects of the project, and the motivation of those involved, to achieve the project objectives within the expected performance targets for time, cost, quality, scope, benefits and risks.

## project management team

The entire management structure of the Project Board, and Project Manager, plus any Team Manager, Project Assurance and Project Support roles.

## project management team structure

An organization chart showing the people assigned to the project management team roles to be used, and their delegation and reporting relationships.

### Project Manager

The person given the authority and responsibility to manage the project on a day-to-day basis to deliver the required products within the constraints agreed with the Project Board.

### project mandate

An external product generated by the authority commissioning the project that forms the trigger for Starting up a Project.

### project office

A temporary office set up to support the delivery of a specific change initiative being delivered as a project. If used, the project office undertakes the responsibility of the Project Support role.

### Project Plan

A high-level plan showing the major products of the project, when they will be delivered and at what cost. An initial Project Plan is presented as part of the Project Initiation Documentation. This is revised as information on actual progress appears. It is a major control document for the Project Board to measure actual progress against expectations.

### Project Support

An administrative role in the project management team. Project Support can be in the form of advice and help with project management tools, guidance, administrative services such as filing, and the collection of actual data.

### quality

The totality of features and inherent or assigned characteristics of a product, person, process, service and/or system that bears on its ability to show that it meets expectations or satisfies stated needs, requirements or specifications.

### quality assurance

An independent check that products will be fit for purpose or meet requirements.

### quality control

The process of monitoring specific project results to determine whether they comply with relevant standards and of identifying ways to eliminate causes of unsatisfactory performance.

### quality criteria

A description of the quality specification that the product must meet, and the quality measurements that will be applied by those inspecting the finished product.

### quality inspection

A systematic, structured assessment of a product carried out by two or more carefully selected people (the review team) in a planned, documented and organized fashion.

### Quality Management Strategy

A strategy defining the quality techniques and standards to be applied, and the various responsibilities for achieving the required quality levels, during a project.

### Quality Register

A register containing summary details of all planned and completed quality activities. The Quality Register is used by the Project Manager and Project Assurance as part of reviewing progress.

## quality review

*See* quality inspection.

## quality review technique

A quality inspection technique with defined roles and a specific structure. It is designed to assess whether a product that takes the form of a document (or similar, e.g. a presentation) is complete, adheres to standards and meets the quality criteria agreed for it in the relevant Product Description. The participants are drawn from those with the necessary competence to evaluate its fitness for purpose.

## request for change

A proposal for a change to a baseline. It is a type of issue.

## reviewer

A person or group independent of the producer who assesses whether a product meets its requirements as defined in its Product Description.

## risk

An uncertain event or set of events that, should it occur, will have an effect on the achievement of objectives. A risk is measured by a combination of the probability of a perceived threat or opportunity occurring, and the magnitude of its impact on objectives.

## risk management

The systematic application of principles, approaches and processes to the tasks of identifying and assessing risks, and then planning and implementing risk responses.

## Risk Management Strategy

A strategy describing the goals of applying risk management, as well as the procedure that will be adopted, roles and responsibilities, risk tolerances, the timing of risk management interventions, the tools and techniques that will be used, and the reporting requirements.

## Risk Register

A record of identified risks relating to an initiative, including their status and history.

## schedule

Graphical representation of a plan (for example, a Gantt chart), typically describing a sequence of tasks, together with resource allocations, which collectively deliver the plan. In PRINCE2, project activities should only be documented in the schedules associated with a Project Plan, Stage Plan or Team Plan. Actions that are allocated from day-to-day management may be documented in the relevant project log (i.e. Risk Register, Daily Log, Issue Register, Quality Register) if they do not require significant activity.

## scope

For a plan, the sum total of its products and the extent of their requirements. It is described by the product breakdown structure for the plan and associated Product Descriptions.

## Senior Responsible Owner

A UK government term for the individual responsible for ensuring that a project or programme of change meets its objectives and delivers the projected benefits. The person should be the owner of the overall business change that is being supported by the project. The Senior

Responsible Owner (SRO) should ensure that the change maintains its business focus, that it has clear authority, and that the context, including risks, is actively managed. This individual must be senior and must take personal responsibility for successful delivery of the project. The SRO should be recognized as the owner throughout the organization.

The SRO appoints the project's Executive (or in some cases may elect to be the Executive)

## Senior Supplier

The Project Board role that provides knowledge and experience of the main discipline(s) involved in the production of the project's deliverable(s). The Senior Supplier represents the supplier interests within the project and provides supplier resources.

## Senior User

The Project Board role accountable for ensuring that user needs are specified correctly and that the solution meets those needs.

## specialist product

A product whose development is the subject of the plan. The specialist products are specific to an individual project (for example, an advertising campaign, a car park ticketing system, foundations for a building, a new business process etc.) Also known as a deliverable or output.

## sponsor

The main driving force behind a programme or project. PRINCE2 does not define a role for the sponsor, but the sponsor is most likely to be the Executive on the Project Board, or the person who has appointed the Executive.

## Sponsoring Group

The driving force behind a programme that provides the investment decision and top-level endorsement for the rationale and objectives of the programme.

## stage

*See* management stage or technical stage.

## Stage Plan

A detailed plan used as the basis for project management control throughout a stage.

## stakeholder

Any individual, group or organization that can affect, be affected by, or perceive itself to be affected by, an initiative (programme, project, activity, risk).

## supplier

The person, group or groups responsible for the supply of the project's specialist products.

## tailoring

The appropriate use of PRINCE2 on any given project, ensuring that there is the correct amount of planning, control, governance and use of the processes and themes (whereas the adoption of PRINCE2 across an organization is known as 'embedding').

## Team Manager

The person responsible for the production of those products allocated by the Project Manager (as defined in a Work Package) to an appropriate quality, timescale and at a cost acceptable to the Project Board. This role reports to, and takes direction from, the Project Manager. If a Team Manager is not assigned, then the Project Manager undertakes the responsibilities of the Team Manager role.

## Team Plan

An optional level of plan used as the basis for team management control when executing Work Packages.

## technical stage

A method of grouping work together by the set of techniques used, or the products created. This results in stages covering elements such as design, build and implementation. Such stages are technical stages and are a separate concept from management stages.

## theme

An aspect of project management that needs to be continually addressed, and that requires specific treatment for the PRINCE2 processes to be effective.

## tolerance

The permissible deviation above and below a plan's target for time and cost without escalating the deviation to the next level of management. There may also be tolerance levels for quality, scope, benefit and risk. Tolerance is applied at project, stage and team levels.

## tranche

A programme management term describing a group of projects structured around distinct step changes in capability and benefit delivery.

## transformation

A distinct change to the way an organization conducts all or part of its business.

## user

The person or group who will use one or more of the project's products.

## Work Package

The set of information relevant to the creation of one or more products. It will contain a description of the work, the Product Description(s), details of any constraints on production, and confirmation of the agreement between the Project Manager and the person or Team Manager who is to implement the Work Package that the work can be done within the constraints.

Index

# Index